One of America's most innovative pastors, Murren has mastered the crucial transition from program-based leadership to process-based leadership. This book will be a critical catalyst for anyone who wants to rekindle vision for ministry in their churches.

Robert R. Redman, Jr.
Director of the Doctor of Ministry Program
Fuller Theological Seminary

Doug is a combat officer leading God's troops to new paradigms where God can bless people through His church. Read this book!

Bruce Larson
Co-pastor, The Crystal Cathedral

They say that the Baby Boomers came back to church, then left. At Doug Murren's church, they came and stayed. Leadership is the X factor in the church of the 21st century. The ideas in **Leadershift** *are battle-tested, biblically based, and on the cutting edge of what we need to know.*

Bob Buford
Founder, Leadership Network

LEADERSHIFT

Doug Murren

Regal Books
A Division of Gospel Light
Ventura, California, U.S.A.

Regal Books
A Division of Gospel Light
Ventura, California, U.S.A.
Printed in U.S.A.

Regal Books is a ministry of Gospel Light, an evangelical Christian
publisher dedicated to serving the local church. We believe God's
vision for Gospel Light is to provide church leaders with biblical, user-
friendly materials that will help them evangelize, disciple and minister
to children, youth and families.

It is our prayer that this Regal Book will help you discover biblical
truth for your own life and help you meet the needs of others. May
God richly bless you.

*For a free catalog of resources from Regal Books/Gospel Light please
contact your Christian supplier or call 1-800-4-GOSPEL.*

Library of Congress Cataloging-in-Publication Data
Murren, Doug, 1951-
    Leadershift / Doug Murren.
        p. cm.
    ISBN 0-8307-1594-0
    1. Pastoral theology. 2. Church management. 3. Christian leadership.
4. Paradigms (Social sciences) I. Title.
    BV4011.M85 1994   94-34881
    253—dc20   CIP

1 2 3 4 5 6 7 8 9 10 11 12 / 00 99 98 97 96 95 94

Rights for publishing this book in other languages are contracted by Gospel
Literature International (GLINT). GLINT also provides technical help for the
adaptation, translation and publishing of Bible study resources and books in
scores of languages worldwide. For further information, contact GLINT, P.O.
Box 4060, Ontario, CA 91761-1003, U.S.A., or the publisher.

CONTENTS

INTRODUCTION

....

I was startled when the phone rang in my private study. Who in the world would call me on my study day? "This had better be good!" I grumbled to myself as I picked up the phone.

"Hello, is this Doug Murren?" blurted the voice on the other end of the line. I didn't recognize it. And few people knew this number.

"Yes," I said quickly, still sliding the phone up my chin.

"My name is Bishop James Smith (the name is changed), and I'd like to talk to you about your influence on one of our pastors," he answered with polite hostility.

"Well okay, go ahead and I'll see if I can address your concerns." I awaited his story with reluctance.

"One of our pastors in Ohio attended one of your seminars on reaching baby boomers and has taken your book *The Baby Boomerang* as a model." He paused. "And he's gotten himself fired. He is one of our best young men and this is a fine church. But, he's stirred up a hornet's nest down there." He cleared his throat as an emotional release.

"Well, what would you like me to do?" I asked. "I'd certainly be willing to give him a call. My intent isn't to get anyone fired." I paused, waiting for him to go on. He didn't continue right away. I really didn't want any bishop mad at me, but neither did I know what I could do about the behavior of someone I didn't even know.

"I would appreciate it if you'd give him a call," the bishop finally said. "I essentially wanted you to know what problems you are raising out there by trying to change churches. But your concern is appreciated." His voice was trembling.

"I'll do what I can." After asking for the pastor's phone number, I hung up the phone and prepared to make the call.

I had suspected there would be some problems with my earlier book and the new discoveries about baby boomers (people born between 1946 and 1964). The Church in the United States had been dominated by the Truman generation (the parents of boomers) for so long it was bound to be tough to make the transition to a new era. And I knew that confronting some of the boomer values would be difficult, too. I had no idea, however, that so many people would have such painful experiences in the change process.

This book offers help in understanding the source of the pain and suggests some remedies. While the focus is on paradigms, the underlying purpose of the book is to help churches reach lost and hurting people—it is a book on evangelism. In my experience, many lost people feel alienated from traditional ways of "doing church." This calls not for compromising the good news, but for better management of our paradigms for outreach and ministry. This book suggests some ways to reposition ourselves so these alienated people can hear us.

NAMING THE PROBLEM

The real culprit in the fight for change is rooted in the often mentioned, but little understood, word "paradigm."

Chapter 1 offers a fairly thorough analysis of this slippery term, so let's pause for only a brief definition here. The word "paradigm" derives from an ancient Greek word *paradeigma*, which simply means "pattern." Although the noun doesn't appear in our New Testaments, the verb form is used in Matthew 1:19. When Joseph discovered that Mary was pregnant before they were married, he determined to discontinue marriage plans quietly, "not willing to make her a publick example" *(KJV)*.

We often use the word "example" to mean a *pattern*. How chaotic life would be without paradigms in this sense! Anyone who wants to please God must pay special attention to *biblical* patterns. I'm sure the bishop who called to protest the influence of my earlier book was concerned that I had not followed biblical paradigms, or patterns, carefully enough.

As I'll also discuss in chapter 1, paradigms do more than give us helpful patterns. They also help shape the way things look to us. For example, if we look at a light through a kaleidoscope, the appearance of the light is affected by the colorful geometric pattern through which we view it.

Now, if you have a kaleidoscope and I don't, we won't see things alike. Anytime two groups hold differing paradigms of reality, conflict is a distinct likelihood. This is what has happened since the Church has tried to discover an effective paradigm, pattern or course of action for reaching baby boomers.

Another source of discomfort and conflict occurs when a favorite paradigm changes—an occurrence that has been given the by-now familiar term "paradigm shift." This kind of disturbance in the way we've grown accustomed to viewing the world can be very disorienting. And it has become a common, if unfortunate, battleground among some church people.

Coming to grips with the nature and function of paradigms is, therefore, crucial both for the Church's faithfulness and for its effectiveness. In order to illustrate our challenge, let me share another recent incident in my life.

"Pastor, the music's too loud here!" The kindly gentleman seemed at ease until I saw the anger dance in his eyes as he walked closer. "And, I don't understand why you speak as though some of the people here don't believe." He paused. I was trying to recall if I knew him. I finally placed his face as someone who had been around the church for a few weeks.

"Well," I explained, "we are trying to develop a congregation for people to whom music is very important to their response to the Lord." I doubted I could satisfy his concerns. I stuck a hand in my pocket and awaited his reply.

"I don't like what you are developing here," the man said. "Are you creating Christians or just some whitewashed environment where they can do what they want?"

"No, actually, I think you just have a different idea about what constitutes good music," I said. "We're expecting that people who don't normally go to church will come with their friends—and they do. We gear part of our presentation for them." I sighed, feeling it was all a little futile.

"Church is for Christians," my questioner replied. "They need to be leading them to Christ before they get here. This is a time for us. And this stuff you are doing is confusing. I'm sure you are a fine pastor, and I enjoy your speaking, but I just can't feel like this is 'home' if this is the way you're going at it." He offered his hand. I shook it and he left.

As has happened frequently lately, I was torn between my pastoral concern for Christians and my passion for the lost. I had to be missing a piece of the puzzle. Why couldn't I get fine people like this man to see what a "seeker-sensitive" church should offer?

NOTABLE PARADIGM SHIFTS

William Carey, the famed missionary, asked the same question in the last century. Carey stood on the docks of England watching the Hudson Bay Company send out its agents to trade for furs and precious metals and other goods around the world. *Eureka!* A thought hit him. *Here was a new pattern for spreading the gospel! The Church needs national representatives, too,* he said to himself. Eventually these representatives would be called "missionaries"—and with his new model, Carey became the greatest missionary pioneer in church history.

Yet, when Carey began presenting his idea to his Christian associates it was not readily accepted. No mental maps or paradigms existed to aid in a discussion of missionizing the world. In fact, the church of Carey's day had little doctrinal or experiential interest in missions.

Patiently and persistently, however, Carey kept saying, "Why *not* send national representatives from the Church to the nations of the world?" Eventually, his new paradigm won acceptance and a pattern for missions was established that would bring countless millions to Christ.

In the mid-1960s the late Dennis Bennett experienced a different paradigm shift, or change in perspective. Although he was an Episcopalian, he became Pentecostal in doctrine, and the modern "charismatic renewal" was born.

The Pentecostal movement and its distinctives had been around since the turn of the century, but it had been a relatively exclusive movement. The idea of mainline churches expressing Pentecostal gifts was certainly unheard of. Yet, Dennis Bennett's message has influenced countless millions in the last two decades. A new model produced new events, and the effect of this change in paradigms is still being felt.

More recently, Bill Hybels looked over the "people-scape" of South Barrington, Illinois, and yet another paradigm shift occurred in the Church. Bill recalls the story of a young high school classmate, who, when invited to Hybels' traditional church, just couldn't relate. The old hymns and formal services seemed to be from another age. Bill decided this wouldn't happen to any of his friends again. He was determined to forge a new format for church, designed for secular, unchurched Americans to understand the message of the gospel.

Hybels' solution was a church for people such as his high school classmate—people he called "Unchurched Harry." It was a novel and radical idea: a church for the unchurched. A church that would be characterized by messages for the unconvinced. A culture that would be "user friendly" to the seeker—the person who sought some connection with Christ but was simply put off by the traditional ways of presenting Him.

Hybels was not seeking to pander to a low level of commitment. His church pioneered a method of approaching church life that would take the thoroughly initiated through a rigorous process of discipleship. But his vision for inviting modern, secular people to discipleship made sense. And by the end of the '80s, his church, Willow Creek Community Church, was described as the largest in the nation.

Facing Realities

I stood in our church services in 1981 and was very concerned about the people in our city who are age 30 and younger. Purportedly, 30 percent of them claimed to be born again, but only 10 percent, or less, actually attended a church in the community. I became convinced we needed a new format that would attract this age group, and younger adults, who were convinced church was irrelevant. We needed a church that would not only *attract* them, but would also *speak* in a relevant way to the lives, questions and fears of baby boomers.

A few key leaders worked with me to develop a format for church that was culturally contemporary. It was "seeker sensitive." But, to my great surprise, not everyone "could see it." As we will see in our study of paradigms, *you only see what you believe*. It was startling for some of our members to see us shift from services focused toward 50- and 60-year-old convinced Christians to 30-year-old largely unconvinced people. We were about to learn how paradigms can blind people to reality.

Our membership dropped from 180 adults to 70. I thought we were finished. But within six months we had an explosion in our midst. Baby boomers began coming in droves. Our new way of expressing evangelism as "Bringing and Including" compelled hundreds and hundreds to begin committing their lives to Christ. This paradigm shift opened up many new and unanticipated opportunities.

WHY WE HAVE TROUBLE WITH PARADIGMS

The agony of dealing with the change needed in churches is exacerbated by the complexity of paradigms. They are tough to take hold of for the following reasons:

- They're subconscious. Most of the time, few of us know we have them.
- They exercise power over us. Convictions of right and wrong are often anchored in our paradigms.
- They're an integral part of our identity.

This brief list of paradigm traits is enough to show why most of us resist change of any kind. Just as Alvin Toffler predicted 30 years ago in his prophetic book *Future Shock*, the level of change most Americans experience is at, or beyond, the toxic level.

Although paradigms can cause us to resist change, this book is based on my conviction that their constructive use is the key to facing change and conflict in churches effectively.

The good news is: Paradigms can be discovered, managed and changed.

Who Should Be Interested in Paradigms?

Do any of these scenarios describe your present set of circumstances?

- Your church has just changed locations, and some of your old-time participants can't understand the new habitat. A typical reaction is, "It's just not the same around here anymore."
- You have accepted a new church, and already you face conflict over what you should be doing as pastor. You really can't determine who is in power. It seems that everybody has a different view of what the church should be.
- You moved from one pastor to two pastors, or from two to three. The church is a little startled and disoriented.
- Your church is experiencing significant conflict over methods, and what the church should do. Everyone seems to have a different notion of the mission on which the church should focus.
- The church is deeply divided over worship styles. A significant number of older members want to stick to traditional hymns, while some younger people want to sing praise songs.

If any of these scenarios sounds like your church, this examination of paradigms should help break the gridlock.

It's only fair that I tell you at the start about my own basic paradigms and perspectives. I am writing as a practitioner. I am neither a sociologist nor a theologian; I am a pastor. I am also a storyteller. Through the grace of God, and the aid of many other fine church leaders, I witnessed the principles in this book help grow the Eastside Foursquare Church in Kirkland, Washington, from a few families to more than 5,000 adherents. My purpose here is to glorify God by sharing the stories behind that growth.

I also write out of the conviction that church folk are going to have to grow in their understanding of paradigms if we want to reach both baby boomers and baby busters (the children of boomers, generally those born between 1965 and 1983), and stay intact. So this book shows how to spot existing paradigms and anticipate new ones. It's about introducing change without creating chaos, and about recognizing when it's best *not* to promote change. It's about dealing with and reducing conflict.

I've included exercises at the end of each chapter to offer a way for you to bring your own experience to this book.

So if you love the Lord and His Church...

if you like a good story...

and if you aren't afraid to wrestle a paradigm to the ground, tame it and harness it for service in the Kingdom, come on along.

1

WHAT IS A PARADIGM?

Understanding the paradigms through which we see life allows a more positive response to change. But first we need to wrap our minds around a clear definition of what a paradigm really is. In his book *Future Edge: Discovering New Paradigms of Success*, Joel Arthur Barker defines a paradigm as, "a set of rules and regulations that: (1) defines boundaries and (2) tells you what to do to be successful within those boundaries."[1]

PARADIGMS AS PATTERNS

Picture the tissue-paper pattern used by a seamstress creating a dress, and you can get an idea of one way a paradigm works. The pattern is made up of a number of pieces that, when pieced together correctly, make a whole dress. The experienced seamstress will lay the fabric out on the table and then place the patterns on the fabric. Next, the fabric is cut precisely according to the pattern. Once the material is all cut out, the dress is sewn together, and *voila*—a dress appears.

Similarly, a paradigm for life is the pattern from which we cut our thinking and behavior. Assembled, they make a cohesive lifestyle.

Our paradigms are also the lenses through which we look at the world. Stephen R. Covey, in his book *Seven Essential Traits of Highly Effective People*, asserts that "Paradigms are powerful because they create the lenses through which we see the world."[2] Like colored glasses, they help determine the way the world appears to us. When several people, such as a church, share these paradigms, they have common views of reality.

PARADIGMS AS LENSES

What You Believe Is What You See

I remember our professor in Psychology 101 trying to teach us about the intricacies of human perception. We discussed the conflicting reports that appear on insurance accident records. He illustrated his point by reading the humorous variations of witness reports regarding the same accident.

Each person who views an accident brings a different perspective to what happened—and, therefore, a different report. Some of the reports even missed the gender of the people involved. Others had nonexistent cars appear from nowhere and do damage. Ever since, I've had trouble trusting the memory!

Some of the reports differed on factors as obvious as race. People of all shades of skin color know the frustration of feeling that others prejudge our attitudes. For America in the '90s, race will have everything to do with the lenses through which we see one another.

My psychology professor convinced me I wasn't a clean

chalkboard waiting for an education to fill it in. I was filled with perceptions. I had models and patterns—paradigms—that helped organize life for me.

The Power of a Paradigm

The experience reminded me of the prophet Elisha and his servant when they were being pursued by their enemies. When Elisha's servant filed his own "incident report," he could say only that he saw the enemy troops and chariots surrounding the city. But Elisha had on different lenses—the lenses of faith. And when, through prayer, he shared that perspective with his servant, "He looked and saw the hills full of horses and chariots of fire all around Elisha" (2 Kings 6:17). Suddenly the servant could see what he believed.

That is the power of a paradigm. As soon as Elisha's servant had a framework in which to put God's forces, he was able to see them. That's the way paradigms work.

Some time ago at one of our church supervisors meetings I began to complain about one of our janitors. "The guy never listens when I talk to him," I said. "In fact, he'll often just walk away from me."

Everyone looked at me with astonishment. Our facilities director gently turned to me and said, "Doug, didn't you know that he is deaf?"

I felt about an inch tall. The next time I saw the young man, I didn't see a recalcitrant custodian. Rather, I saw a remarkable young man who was very good at reading lips. My new paradigm allowed me to see him in a new light. My shift in perception allowed him to grow in my eyes.

Paradigms in Conflict

You have a set of paradigms for your congregation—lenses

through which you see its leaders and its congregational life. You also have a definition of *what makes a successful church life*. However, multiple dozens, possibly even hundreds, of other conflicting paradigms are at work in the life of your church that can result in conflict, such as occurred in one of my early church experiences.

My First Home Church

I strode into the little Pentecostal church, behind my friend Don. I had never seriously attended church before, so I was nervous. Don had told me I'd "dig the music." "It's just like a black church," he said. I finally found the courage to attend when several friends agreed to come with us.

My friend Tim bounded up the steps first, stomping the snow off his feet. Together we looked like the remains of Woodstock. The smell of patchouli oil lingered in the air behind us as we moved through the foyer into the sanctuary. I'm sure the people there could have described us as hippies.

I loved the service, and so did all my friends. Within weeks, 60 to 75 of us young college kids were attending the service. We were all in various stages of deliverance from drugs and what not. But we grew to really love this church. The pastor was totally different from us, but he had a great way of relating to young people. I see now that he was a bold and courageous leader. He made no effort whatsoever to change the way we dressed, or to re-create us in the image of the previous, older, members.

Eventually, the pastor introduced the music we liked into the services. Not long afterward, we began to feel the tension. Soon the older members of the church sat on one side of the room and the newer people on the other. I got a sense of what was happening after one of the services, when I overheard Sister Melva and her husband "pitchin' a fit" with the pastor.

"We can't allow these girls comin' here dressed like you let them," they complained. "And my goodness, you can't tell the girls from the boys."

The pastor didn't respond, but you could see his ears redden.

"This ungodly music is terrible," Sister Melva continued. "The bass player isn't even hitting the right notes. (I was the bass player.) I'm telling you, Pastor, we can't tolerate this."

We found out later that the older group of church members had given the pastor an ultimatum: *"It's either us or them!"* He told them he would choose the 1 sheep who was lost over the 99 who were already found.

Does this happen today? I think so. I hear angry talk about drama, church marketing and the nature of church music from people who were considered controversial themselves just a decade or two ago. What's happening? The rules—the paradigms—are always changing. Not the important rules of grace, the divinity of Christ, His death, burial and resurrection and the authority of Scripture, but the less important rules of methodology. Here's a recent example.

A Question of Leadership

I usually make my rounds through our church facilities once or twice a week. I like to hear about the issues our supervisors are facing. We seem to have no shortage of crises. One day I wanted to meet with Wayne (not his real name), a member of our pastoral team. He had left a note, begging for some time with me.

"Hey, Wayne, what's happening?" I asked, plopping myself into the chair in front of his desk.

"We've got a problem with another church in town about one of our singles leaders," Wayne said. He was scrambling around in his briefcase for the sheet of paper containing the details.

He handed it to me and I read through it quickly. A church

was objecting to our placing a woman who had been divorced in a trusted position with single leaders. Her ex-husband attended their church, and he was offended by it.

"Man, I hate these things," I grumbled.

"What do we want to do? Do you want to meet with the pastor?" Wayne asked, even though he knew I hated inter-church conflict.

"No, I don't think so," I sighed. "Don't you think you can take care of it?"

"What do you want me to do? Take her from leadership? You know her 'ex' beat her up pretty badly. I checked it out. She even got sole custody of the kids for some time. We have similar situations in our group, you know," Wayne said.

I paused to think, then said bluntly, "We can't take her from leadership."

"They say they're going to take this very seriously," Wayne countered. "They're very strict about divorce. They don't let anyone lead who has ever been divorced. They think we're soft. Do you think we can make peace with them?" Wayne stood up from his desk and walked over to his file cabinet.

"How can they hold to that view when a majority of people these days are divorced—or just living together, for that matter?" I asked rhetorically. "We're living in different times." I suppose I hoped this statement would resolve the problem.

"You know, it's a matter of viewpoint," Wayne said. "We view divorcees as victims. They see them as perpetrators. We see a leader as someone who has made mistakes—someone who has been healed to help others. They see leaders as models, called to hold up standards. I don't really think we are going to come together on this one."

Wayne stopped, then added, "I'll take care of it the best I can, but I don't think we can avoid some bad feelings. She is a great person and I'm certain she's been called as a leader. She's really broken up by the whole thing."

Relieved, I said, "Okay, Wayne. I appreciate it." And I left his office toward the safer realm of the music department.

Wayne was right on target. What we had here were two different viewpoints, two different paradigms—each with a part

NOT ONLY DO PARADIGMS SERVE AS LENSES AND PATTERNS, THEY ARE ALSO THE RULES BY WHICH WE PLAY THE GAME OF LIFE. CHURCHES HAVE RULES THAT DICTATE HOW WE PLAY THE GAME OF "CHURCH LIFE."

of the truth. At this point, I'm not so interested in arguing that we had the better part, but in pointing out the necessity of leaders who can see how differing perceptions affect congregational life. Good leaders of the future will use paradigms to prepare congregations for effectiveness in a quickly changing and complex world.

PARADIGMS AS RULES OF THE GAME

Not only do paradigms serve as lenses and patterns, they are also the rules by which we play the game of life. Churches have rules that dictate how we play the game of "Church Life." Sometimes churches are forced to change the way they play. It is usually during times of change that we run headlong into the need to reexamine our rules.

Keeping Things Cricket

Let me illustrate. Both basketball and football are games that use a ball. Both also have a referee, uniforms, fans and two competing teams. Yet they are very different games. If you intend to play basketball by football rules, you will foul out of the game before the first time-out. If you try to play football with basketball rules, you'll have a little trouble bouncing the ball. And...well, you see what I mean. It gets absurd.

Several years ago, I was invited to attend a conference in England. Our hosts booked a room for me in a very nice inn near the Heathrow Airport in London. Every day, our afternoons were free. I did my exercise regimen by swimming a bit, then returned to my room.

I began to flip through the "telly" channels to get an idea of what English TV was like. I was especially intrigued by a cricket match being televised. This particular match was an important one—a championship game. One of the teams was from Australia and the other was from northern England. The competition was intense, and the crowd was very involved.

My short respite at the television set was interrupted when the conference leader came to take me to the meeting. The next afternoon during my free time, I returned to the TV and, to my surprise and confusion, a cricket match was on again— and it appeared, remarkably, like the match I watched the day before.

At first I assumed it had to be a rerun. Yet, the scores were very different from what they had been the day before. Sure enough, this match was, obviously, the same game. What kind of game *is* this? I asked myself. I couldn't imagine watching a baseball game that continued overnight! I had no paradigm to understand the game of cricket.

I *had* to understand this game! I changed out of my exercise clothes and headed down to the bar in search of someone to explain the game to me. The men in the bar got quite a kick out of the fact that I was a minister. They got an even bigger kick out of my inability to comprehend the essence of cricket. One fellow said, "You Yanks just can't get the game, fella."

A big, blonde truck driver with a skeleton tattooed on his hand decided to "have a go" at explaining the game. Every time he would attempt to explain a facet of the game I would brighten up and say, "You mean something like baseball?" Frustrated, he would shake his head and mumble, "No, no, no. Forget baseball. This is cricket."

I, obviously, had no existing paradigm and understood no set of rules that allowed me to understand this new game. The best I could do was attempt to bend cricket into the mold of games I already understood and enjoyed.

Eventually, however, by sticking to it patiently, the new rules began to make sense. I experienced an "Aha, Eureka!" kind of moment, when cricket suddenly became not "sort of like baseball" but, well, *cricket*—a game distinct in its own right. I owned the "cricket zone."

When Football Isn't Football

I have an Australian friend who likes to talk sports. One frosty fall afternoon we were talking about his illustrious high school sports career. Grant told me he had been a standout halfback in football.

Now, being thoroughly American, I didn't realize that "football" was the name for soccer in Australia. I, subsequently, visualized Grant participating in the "he-man" American game with all the pads, grunting and groaning, pounding his bulky teammates into the dirt.

"So, you like football, huh Grant?" I said.

"You bet," he grinned. "I played championship halfback in Australia."

"I didn't know they played football in Australia!" I said.

"You bet!" Grant exclaimed. "In fact, it's the top national sport."

"I thought rugby was the big game there," I said, trying to get a rise out of him.

"Rugby is a bit of a crude game. Some of the toughs play it, but the real game of precision is football," he returned.

I mulled over the irony of football being a contest of "precision." It struck me that although Grant was discussing what he knew to be football, he really meant soccer. Simultaneously, we discovered our miscommunication and had a good laugh about it.

Grant's paradigm was soccer. My paradigm was Monday Night Football. Both games involve a team. Both teams have a halfback, and both halfbacks handle a ball. In both games, the object is to move the ball downfield toward a goal. Both games are also called "football." But, in actuality, they are two vastly different games.

Toward a Common Vision of Church

I believe this is how we come to understand the gospel. When I first heard the gospel, I had a difficult time understanding concepts such as heaven and hell. I found the idea of God too expansive, and the story of Christ dying for my sins too far beyond my experience. But one day someone said the right phrase. I believe it was something like, "Jesus Christ died to show you He was your friend." The idea of friendship triggered concepts I already knew, understood and valued; and I said, "Aha! I can understand that." The "right" phrase served as a new paradigm—a way of understanding what Christ has done for me.

This is how it often works in church life, too. Our early definitions of church stay with us for a lifetime. People in the church often don't catch a new church vision because they are playing by the rules they learned long ago. But many of them are waiting for us to strike a harmonious chord in their hearts. They may sense that this new game of church is potentially interesting and even exciting, but until they are given a way to connect with the new methods, arguing with them or shouting at them will be nothing but an absurd contest.

Back at my home church, the older members could not understand that people who were different might want to

ONLY BY DEVELOPING A COMMON PARADIGM CAN A CHURCH MARCH FORWARD WITH A COMMON FOCUS.

come to church. They had no rules for hippies "playing church." Other churches have similar paradigm problems. If the rules say worship time is at 11:00 sharp on Sunday morning, then you will run into trouble if you try to have the singing at another time—unless you first offer a way to make this paradigm shift. In other churches, if the pastor never wears a tie in the service, he may seem a little outside the rules if he chooses to wear one

Again, we may use words such as church, ministry and preaching, while being unaware of the multiple definitions of these terms, depending on the experiences of those who hear them. Our words might lead us to believe we are playing the same game by the same rules, but if contradictory definitions of purpose and methods exist, we are not communicating effectively. It's a little like the apostle Paul's warning:

> Unless you speak intelligible words with your tongue, how will anyone know what you are say-

ing? You will just be speaking into the air....If then I do not grasp the meaning of what someone is saying, I am a foreigner to the speaker, and he is a foreigner to me (1 Cor. 14:9-11).

It is vital that the leader begin to spot the appearance of subtle, but paralyzingly divergent, notions about the rules of the game. Only by developing a common paradigm can a church march forward with a common focus. The point, of course, is rarely whose rules are right. The point is that unless members can agree to play by the same rules, churches will rarely rise to great fruitfulness.

Our age requires that we be "paradigm aware." Today's effective communicator must take the lead in promoting an understanding of how our paradigm affects the way we define and "do" church.

THE IMPACT OF PARADIGMS

Let's review the significance of paradigms.

- Paradigms lay out a pattern for life, and give us boundaries within which to define success.
- Paradigms provide a lens through which we observe reality.
- Paradigms establish the rules and definitions of the game we are playing, and get us all on the same page.
- Paradigms give structure and meaning to our actions.
- Paradigms allow us to move ahead into our future with a common focus as a group. They enable us to expend resources more efficiently, avoid

"quenching the Spirit" (see 1 Thess. 5:19, *KJV*) as
a congregation, and release more of His power.

Our congregations are joyous places to serve when we are
all observing reality through the same lens, playing by the
same rules and cutting our success out of the same pattern.
I've spoken in enough different churches to know that
although local customs must be taken very seriously, many
good and honest hearts are waiting to be shown the value of
new methods. Fruitfulness for many unfruitful churches is only
one paradigm shift away.

PARADIGMS *in* PRACTICE

1. Make a list of everything you can think of that football
and basketball have in common, and another list of their differences. Looking at the two lists, decide whether it would be
easier for a football player to "shift paradigms" and learn basketball, or vice versa.

2. Have you ever experienced church conflict that could be
attributed to members operating by differing rules or paradigms? First, name the difficulty. Then see if you can write a
specific set of rules—the paradigm—followed by each side of
the controversy.

3. Scripture presents some paradigms that are nonnegotiable. Describe as briefly as possible the firm principles taught
in the following passages.

   a. 1 Corinthians 15:3,4
   b. Galatians 2:15,16,21
   c. Galatians 5:16-21

Notes

1. Joel Arthur Barker, *Future Edge: Discovering New Paradigms of Success* (New York: William Morrow and Company, 1992), p. 14.
2. Stephen R. Covey, *Seven Essential Traits of Highly Effective People* (New York: Simon and Schuster, 1989), p. 32.

2

....

TEAM BUILDING THROUGH PARADIGMS

You may be asking, What difference do paradigms really make in the actual life of the Church? What difference, if any, do they make in the way you and your ministry team exercise leadership?

Simply put, paradigms can make the difference between a church that, on the one hand, is wandering aimlessly (or following a dozen different visions), and, on the other hand, a church that has a single focus and is supportive of its leaders because it shares their vision.

DISSONANT VISIONS OF LEADERSHIP

Catching Up, Catching On

Take, for example, the apostle Peter and the others on Christ's ministry team. Jesus' "paradigm" for His mission, and theirs, was one that involved self-sacrifice. At first, the apostles did not share that vision:

> He then began to teach them that the Son of Man
> must suffer many things and be rejected by the
> elders, chief priests and teachers of the law, and that
> he must be killed and after three days rise again. He
> spoke plainly about this, and Peter took him aside
> and began to rebuke him (Mark 8:31,32).

Peter's paradigm of the Messiah was of a conquering hero.
The last thing he envisioned was a "suffering Servant" kind of
Messiah. Only after he betrayed his Lord, only after Jesus'
death on the cross and subsequent resurrection, did Peter
catch the vision. And when he did, he was transformed from
a follower too frightened to admit that he knew Jesus, to an
outspoken proclaimer of the good news, and became a self-
sacrificial leader himself.

If your congregation doesn't share your vision, they will
feel a dissonance between what you are asking them to commit to and their own expectations of themselves, and of you.
It is essential that they understand your paradigm if you
expect to count on them to help you steer the ship. Once they
do, incredible power is released.

As leaders, we have the challenge of being aware that the
expectations people have of us will be determined by the
framework of how they believe a good leader looks and acts.
While contending for your own self-identity, it is also necessary to understand the expectations of those you lead. Once a
leader is aware of the image his charge has of a leader, it is
important to use that awareness to develop common paradigms. Paradigm awareness can help leaders avoid becoming
victims of unspoken expectations.

A Gardener-Leader
My wife and I were part of a team of young people with the
Youth With a Mission outreach in the Munich Olympics in

1971. We sold everything we had to get there. It was an exciting experience to watch God provide at every turn.

We were encouraged to do a fair amount of reading before we went. One of the books that struck us most was Brother Andrew's book *God's Smuggler.* We were both captivated by his adventures behind the Iron Curtain. This was in the early '70s, when those nations represented a formidable obstacle to sharing the gospel.

Because we were part of a musical group planning to do outreach in Denmark before the events began in Munich, we arrived a few weeks before the many other teams coming from all over the world. Our feet were on European soil no more than five minutes before we were off to a small Bible college in the center of Denmark.

Weary from the long flight and an eight-hour drive, we stumbled down the rubber-covered bus steps into the entrance of the Bible college.

"Hi, kids! Can I help you?" offered a small man dressed in work clothes.

"Sure," I said, handing him my carry-on bag. *The gardener is a nice man,* I thought to myself. This kind man continued to help us for about an hour. He also carried our large speaker cabinets. None of us really offered much respect. We assumed gardeners were supposed to help out. He could have been the head janitor, for all we knew.

We were all excited about the evening meeting, although we were dog-tired. We had been told that Brother Andrew was addressing the whole student body, and we were the invited guests.

As we entered the auditorium, it became obvious that a number of people from town had heard the news, too. The room was jammed. We sang a lot of action-type songs, and as we waved our uplifted hands and jumped around some, the crowded room grew hotter.

After our rousing worship time, the head of the Bible school stood up and went to the podium. "Tonight it is my privilege to introduce a great friend and great man," he said. "Brother Andrew."

To our surprise, the "gardener" stepped up to the platform. He smiled in our direction.

When we had first seen him upon our arrival, Brother Andrew did not fit my picture of a leader. I had missed the fact that he exhibited a principle of true, godly leadership—helping graciously without giving himself the credit of an introduction. The experience broadened my definition of a real leader. Brother Andrew's example had provided me with a shift in my "leadership paradigm." I shared his vision, learning that a leader can wear gardener's clothes.

Paradigm Tension

Our congregation has an aggregate attendance of 5,000 people. Many of our congregants have a "paradigm set" that works well with 250 people. Tensions often arise when it strikes home that a church of 5,000 does very few things the same as a church of 250.

Occasionally, I'll putter around in our on-site bookstore about an hour before our worship services. I like to get away from the intensity of the worship team preparation.

One Sunday morning in the bookstore, I met a handsome couple about my age—in their early 40s. "Hi, Pastor! My name is John and this is my wife, Louise," the husband said as he extended his hand in greeting.

"How are you?" I responded. "I don't think we have met before...have we?" My mind raced as I tried to recall whether I knew this couple.

"No, we're new. We've come from California," John offered.

Then his wife spoke up. "At our last church, we often had our pastor over for dinner. Would you and your wife be free this Saturday night?" Louise was happy to offer a gracious invitation.

I knew I was going to have to be gentle. This happens to me about three times a month. Being such an introvert, I am usually struck first with a siege of panic at such invitations. Then I get more rational and answer the question.

"You know," I said, "Deb and I just can't do that. There are really two reasons. First, we are committed to service activities three nights out of the week, and we've tried to make it a rule to be home four nights a week. Second, our congregation has close to 2,500 families in it. We'd be dead by Christmas if we tried to accept such invitations."

"Oh...we can see that," John said. "But how do you get to know everyone?" He looked quizzical.

"I don't," I said. "We have hundreds of lay pastors, dozens of home-group leaders and about 25 full-time pastors who make calls and visits." I hoped this might be encouraging.

"Well, that just doesn't seem like a church to me," John replied.

"I don't think I'd want to be counseled or prayed for by a layperson or pastor who wasn't 'feeding me,'" Louise added.

"When you say 'feeding,' do you mean preaching?" I wanted to make sure I got her point, but I'd also admit to a bit of sarcasm in my reply.

"Yes," she replied.

"Well, we have developed a little different approach here. You might try our Church 101 class to get acquainted with it," I encouraged.

"I don't know," John interrupted. "I think what my wife is saying is that we wanted to be a part of a church. This is a bit different for us." That was clearly the end of the dialogue as far as he was concerned. But I wanted to take it just a little further.

"See, we believe our cause and mission and the Lord are the unifying factors around here—not me," I explained. "If I can help clarify anything more, please let me know. I'd be happy to. See you again, I hope." I walked out of the bookstore a little sorry I had ventured in.

Explanations Versus Judgments

Obviously, John and Louise and I we were on different wavelengths in defining a church. Our conflicting experience was based on differing paradigms of what defines a pastor, pastoral care and the church. Yet, I was careful not to label this couple's expectations as "wrong." Thinking in terms of paradigms is much more constructive than thinking in terms of right and wrong. Still, getting everyone on the same wavelength is a formidable task.

CHURCH HEALTH REQUIRES THAT ITS LEADERS ALL HOLD THE SAME "PICTURE" OF A COMPLETED CHURCH.

It helps to clarify your own vision. In my case, being able to state the difference between a 250-member church's view of a leader and that of a 5,000-member church is essential. I face these same kinds of issues at each stage of our church growth. I focus on being able to articulate the new paradigm required for the next stage, not only in order to communicate it clearly, but also to be able to state it objectively instead of passing judgment on alternatives—which can lead to personal grudges.

Being able to articulate paradigm conflicts is rewarding in our task as leaders. Paradigm awareness helps us ferret out the need for paradigm education. In every one of our church leadership training seminars I try to deal with a wide variety of the possible paradigms available to churches, then clarify the paradigms to which our church holds. This gives people permission to decide if they want to adhere to our paradigm set or not, without any one person being a "bad guy." If they choose not to, that is a viable and reasonable choice for them to make. But it is much more unifying if this choice is made beyond a subconscious and emotional level.

PARADIGM SETS

Paradigms often appear in *sets*. They gather in our brain something like molecules. Many smaller portions such as atoms make up the big picture. A paradigm set that defines a church could include the following areas:

- The definition of a good leader;
- The role of a church board;
- The decision-making process;
- What constitutes a worship service;
- The definition of adequate facilities;
- The purpose of the church;
- The definition of paid staff and how it relates to other church leadership;
- How church membership is defined and maintained;
- The definition of the aim of worship.

Our overall paradigm of what we mean by church includes *at least* all these subareas. Paradigm sets make up the large picture. Differing paradigm sets defining what we mean by "church" can cause collisions all over the place. Church health requires that its leaders all hold the same "picture" of a completed church.

A Paradigm Confrontation

It was a Monday night and I was headed for a meeting with members of a new church we had planted about two hours away. Intense difficulty had paralyzed this young church. I dreaded the trip. I hate meetings that are called for the specific purpose of having a confrontation. And I'm always exhausted after preaching all day Sunday. Fortunately, my church consultant friend Dr. Lucky Klopp went with me.

As we pulled in the driveway of the home where we were to meet, we could see that the house was full. I was already feeling myself get edgy. A friend opened the door and invited us in. "Come on in and grab a seat. I think most of the people are here," he said. Lucky walked in ahead of me. We gestured a greeting to everyone. We had become very well acquainted with the people over the last several months, and we loved them dearly.

"Well, why don't I begin?" I said as I took a sip of fruit punch. (I hate the stuff, but I've sure had my share at church meetings and weddings.) "I understand we've got some problems here. As I hear it, you don't like Bill (not his real name) as pastor. This really surprises me. You've seen people meet Christ under Bill's preaching. I think he is one of the best pastors I've ever seen." I stopped and leaned back on the couch.

After a minute that passed as slowly as two hours, a large contractor named Steve dared to speak. "Our problem is the way decisions are made."

"What kind of decisions?" Lucky asked quickly.

"Well, like which worship choruses we sing, and who will lead small groups. We aren't into following *man* here"—indicating a strong aversion to one-man decision making. Half the people in the room nodded in agreement.

Lucky responded that we understood their background was congregational, while ours was appointive. "But we explained in the beginning that the pastor makes those kinds of decisions as part of his role," he said, leaning forward and taking a sip of coffee.

"We didn't realize it would be so different from our background," a young mother contributed. "We wanted this to be more of a team-led church."

"Well, then you should have spoken up before we got the church started, so we could have clarified that," I said. "I think you guys are great people. I was very excited about the church. Most people in your position don't feel we do enough—but here it seems that we've done too much." Only a few nodded in agreement.

"I think we'd better close the church down because there is already just too much conflict," I concluded. "I think we have too many ideas of what was supposed to be happening. Let's part friends. Your pastor can regroup, and you can think about starting a church that is congregationally ruled."

We all agreed on the plan to discontinue the church. Then we shared ice cream and cookies.

I have thought about this situation many times. I wished I had taken time to take this group through a discussion of what they believed a church is. They are good people, and we all deserved to have our differing paradigm sets for church clarified. Simply walking through a polite statement and doctrinal overview isn't enough when there are competing models of what a church at work should look like.

This process of paradigm clarification is a never-ending journey. Certain junctures in church growth are most excruciating. The threshold between a 400- and a 700-member church is one critical juncture. I would advise professional consultation for any church breaking this barrier. Whatever the present size of your church, significant changes in approach or numbers are bound to cause crises. As an occasional church consultant, I have come to realize that most conflict in churches stems from unclarified paradigms, paradigm tampering or difficult paradigm shifts.

PARADIGMS AND PRIORITIES

What Is a Pastor?
A good exercise for you as a church leader is to write down 20 tasks you believe a pastor should do at your church. Then take another sheet and make a list of those personality traits

---

PARADIGMS FUNCTION AS THE LENSES THROUGH WHICH WE SEE CHURCH. WE SEE WHAT WE BELIEVE, AND THEN WE SAY, "YES, THIS IS 'CHURCH.'"

---

that are essential for a pastor to have. (See the exercise at the end of this chapter.)

As soon as you have completed these lists, call at least five key laypersons in your church. Say, "Hi, could you do a little exercise for me? Over the next three days would you list 20 tasks a pastor should do at our church, then another list of the personality traits your first list requires? And would you mail the lists to my office sometime this week?"

I predict you will be astonished by the variety of paradigm sets you receive, and the pastoral priorities they indicate. These priorities grow out of the paradigms people hold of what they expect a church to be.

Once again: Paradigms function as the lenses through which we see church. We see what we believe, and then we say "Yes, this is 'church.'"

What Is a Successful Church?

Paradigms also define success. Coloring outside the lines of the church's definition of success can quickly get a pastor into trouble. It is important that these boundaries be consistent.

Going back to the example of a football game, if we are going to play soccer we must all agree to play by soccer rules rather than by football rules. Even when everyone on the field agrees that the thick chalk lines mark out-of-bounds, you won't have much of a soccer game if when the whistle blows one fellow keeps trying to take the ball and throw it to a teammate.

Pastors and laypersons can make lists of what they expect of the church that are similar to the previous exercise on pastors. If your lists differ vastly, could you possibly make adjustments in order to harmonize them? Can you identify any fundamental assumptions, expectations or priorities that may be contributing to your differences?

This exercise also applies if you happen to be a leader of a ministry within, or other than, a church. Take your key volunteers and ask them to define your role as their leader. Also, ask them to make a list of 10 to 20 points describing how they perceive the purpose and mission of your organization. Then create your own list and, as with the other examples, check for similarities and differences. You should begin to see how each list is the product of differing lenses that affect a person's view of ministry.

AVOIDING PARADIGM COLLISIONS

A clear statement of a church's purpose is a significant step toward developing a common vision—a common paradigm set. A purpose statement reveals to all, "This is what we mean by 'church!'" It is an essential piece of information for anyone who wants to run out on the field and participate. More fundamentally, it helps people to consider joining the team.

We use a four-week course called Church 101 to communicate what we mean by "church" at Eastside. It is our finding that congregations who have implemented similar classes are very effective, for the simple reason that when the church's purpose is clarified, everyone has a common sense of its aim—and a picture of what the church looks like when it is "successful."

At Eastside, we also do monthly Volunteer Leadership Training Seminars. During these seminars, I often field questions from the floor. At these sessions, it's revealing to ask for five-word definitions of what people believe a church is. This is an effective way to test for potential paradigm collision courses.

The primary aim of our Church 101 class is to encourage our members to accept the paradigm that matches our mission. However, if we planned to avoid all paradigm collisions simply by informing the minority who attend these meetings, we would be in trouble. So to teach the rest of the adherents our style and purpose, we regularly share some of our church "folklore" in our services. Anecdotal stories and teachings about the mission and purpose of our church clarify the mission of Eastside. All these tactics are aimed at avoiding paradigm collisions.

Patterns of Ministry

Definitions of what we mean by ministry or worship haven't always been communicated as clearly as I would like to think.

Let me share with you an instance where an approach to pastoral care introduced me to the world of "ministry patterns."

I had known the young, spiritually alive couple I was about to meet in the office for quite some time. During the weeks preceding the appointment, I had detected a great deal of stress in the wife's countenance. As I waited for them to arrive, I wondered to myself why they were so anxious to see me.

My phone intercom buzzed as my office assistant informed me that Jim, the husband, was on the phone.

He began anxiously. "Pastor, we can't make it to your office, but you need to come over. Shelley has locked herself in the bathroom and says that I have been found unworthy and the angels are coming to get me."

Right then, as I headed for the door, my mind raced about the many ways this situation could be handled. The way a pastor approaches this sort of crisis says a great deal about his paradigm of care. Some people would do an exorcism. I could suspect that Jim was actually abusing Shelley. (Another might take Shelley's claim that the angels were coming as a good reason to stay as far away from the house as possible!)

In less than 15 minutes, I found myself striding apprehensively up the creaky, wooden steps leading to their front door. Each step made my heart beat faster. I really cared for this couple, and I prayed inwardly that I would indeed be able to help them.

"Hi Jim," I said, embracing him in compassion when he opened the door. Shelley had moved to the dining room.

"Pastor," Jim began, "she is in here praying for me and she says she is holding the angels back." He hung his head.

Looking in Shelley's direction, I asked her hesitantly, "Shelley...how are you doing?"

"Not so well, Doug," she wept.

"How about if we go to the doctor and see if he can help us?" I ventured, hoping she would stay lucid enough to trust me.

"She hasn't slept in I don't know how long," Jim explained, as he helped Shelley out to my car.

We placed Shelly in the local psychiatric ward of our city's hospital. She was diagnosed as manic-depressive and the doctor prescribed lithium. Within a month, the couple had scheduled another appointment with me.

"Doug, do you think Christians should take psychiatric drugs?" Jim asked during this second appointment. "Shelley's uncle, who is a minister, says that if she just comes to grip with her fears, God will help her. He also encouraged us to let you minister to us."

"Shelley, what do you think?" I asked in return.

"Well," she began, "I feel better taking the drugs, but growing up I was taught against psychiatrists and psychology in general."

"Jim, what do you think?" I looked at him, hopeful that he would help the conversation but unsure whether he would.

"Well, she is definitely better. But I don't know—maybe she just needs to be stronger or just get more sleep," Jim responded. His tone of voice indicated he was not sold on the medication.

"Would you guys think it was unchristian if I took insulin for diabetes?" I posed the question and waited.

"Oh no," they both answered.

"Lithium is just a salt that balances brain chemistry," I explained.

I went on, in effect explaining that a paradigm for ministry can sometimes trap us and exclude us from allowing certain kinds of help. "I believe medicine can be viewed as a gift from God," I said. "I also believe in doing anything that's helpful if the Bible doesn't prohibit it. If I were you, I'd take this medicine and praise God for it. I believe that it's ministering to you in a deep way, and I'm praying for you."

As they left the office, I was so glad they had received the right professional help. Our limited paradigm of care in ministry often keeps us from effectively helping people. This is unfortunate. A paradigm that says, Yes, physical healing is needed as well as spiritual healing, allows qualified people to identify problems and offer help.

I have learned to train my staff in a "holistic" approach to care—a model that understands that the medical, emotional and spiritual realms all overlap. I believe this fits "biblical anthropology"—Scripture's definition of people as composed of an interrelated body, soul and spirit (see 1 Thess. 5:23). We expect leaders who desire to be a part of our ministry team to accept this paradigm for ministry.

The reason for this is simple. A multiminister team must be carefully built on a common foundation and grow out of a shared philosophy. Ministry is too sacred a task, too crucial a charge, to allow serious paradigm collisions to surprise you.

PARADIGMS *in* PRACTICE

1. Make a list of 20 tasks you expect of a pastor. Then, across from each task, write down the personal quality or trait required to carry out that task.

2. Reflecting on the attitude of most of the people in your congregation, put a check mark beside each task on your list that you believe they would also list. Add any tasks you think they would list, that you did not. Does the result indicate a paradigm gap you should check on by actually surveying the congregation in order to eliminate guesswork?

3. Make another list of the qualities Paul taught should characterize leaders in the Early Church (see 1 Tim. 3:1-12; Titus 1:6-9). Which of these qualities do you, and any other leaders in your church, need to work on?

3

WHEN PARADIGMS COLLIDE

Recently, I took a great risk as a leader—one that resulted in a collision between two views of what the Church should be and do. To me, the incident shows that paradigm collisions need not be destructive, and that it's essential to know when it's worth it to risk a confrontation.

LOVING WITHOUT STRINGS

Having become convinced that we as Christians need to reexamine our attitude toward our Jewish and Old Covenant roots, I invited my good friend Rabbi Yechiel Eckstein, founder and president of the Fellowship of Jews and Christians, to speak to our congregation.

My friendship with Yechiel has been very rewarding. Surprisingly, he has taught me a good deal about evangelism. I asked him one day, "Yechiel, do you ever get annoyed hanging around us Christians when you know any one of us would consider it the ultimate prize to convert you?"

He replied, "No, I am here to show you Christians how the gospel is supposed to work. As I read in your New Testament, you are supposed to love other people—and leave the converting to the Holy Spirit." *Not a bad message,* I thought, so I invited Yechiel to speak at our church.

Following his visit, a concerned young man came and asked me, "Was that guy a Christian?"

"No," I said with a grin.

"Well, why did he speak?" My questioner wasn't grinning. He wanted a full explanation.

"Well," I explained, "I feel that we need to know more about our Jewish roots. The Church's roots are in Israel. Now, I wouldn't have just anybody speak to you. But Yechiel's ministry is allowing Christians to discover their roots and allowing Jews to get over their fear of Christians." I awaited his reaction.

"But what about commitment to what we believe?" I could tell he feared that we had left the faith.

"See, I believe that commitment without tolerance destroys, and tolerance without commitment makes us worse. We've had a rare opportunity to bless a leader of God's chosen people. And, who knows, if we love Yechiel, perhaps he will discover Jesus as his Messiah. But even if he doesn't, we love him unconditionally." I hoped the inquisition was over.

It wasn't.

"But, if we weren't trying to evangelize him, why did you have him here?" the young man insisted, sitting down on the arm of a chair.

"I had him here to illustrate the paradigm of love," I said. "Love is unconditional. It is love without an agenda—the kind God has. We American Christians are certain that if we don't do everything with an end-product in mind, we've wasted our time. Yechiel helped us today. He tested our perception of reality, and for that I'm thankful."

"I can see that," the young man said. He nodded his head in thanks and headed out the side door.

Fortunately, this paradigm collision had an amicable outcome. Even if it hadn't, the issue was important enough for me

....

RISK TAKING IS A VITAL INGREDIENT FOR LEADERS. COPING WITH CRITICISM IS A NEEDED SKILL IF WE ARE TO BOLDLY GO WHERE THE CHURCH HAS NEVER GONE BEFORE.

....

to risk a confrontation. Risk taking is a vital ingredient for leaders. Coping with criticism is a needed skill if we are to boldly go where the Church has never gone before.

DARING TO BE A DANIEL

In our day, paradigm collisions are inevitable because we have so many models of church. Sometimes this occurs when believers move and must find a new church home. In large cities, believers acting as consummate consumers float among denominational groups and churches of different sizes. This sets the stage for prolific paradigm collisions.

None of these cultural confrontations is as radical as that faced by the Old Testament hero Daniel.

Scene: The training school of Nebuchadnezzar (see Daniel 1).
Date: Passover, 607 B.C.

Daniel: "Shadrach, we will not be celebrating Passover this year. How does a Jew celebrate deliverance when he is a captive?"

Shadrach: "Maybe there are no more Jews."

Daniel: "What is a Jew? Those of privilege who seek special positions in the court? Schemers who have sold out to the Babylonians so they can continue to thrive as traders?"

Shadrach: "No! *We* are the Jews! A Jew is one who is loyal to the God of Israel."

Daniel: "You are right. A Jew is not just a Jew in Zion. We are Jews. A Jew is one who keeps himself loyal to Jacob's God. We are Jews! And we must find what it means to be a Jew in a captive land. This is God's message—being a Jew is bigger than gazing upon the walls of His holy city."

Shadrach: "How will we be Jews?"

Daniel: "We will start by not eating meat offered to idols of other gods. God will honor this. When we are old and gone, others will read and see that being a Jew was from within. God be praised forever!"

The book of Daniel shows a band of loyal followers facing a collision in paradigms. Though small in number, they were strategically placed. They defined anew the meaning of what it meant to be Jewish. Daniel and his friends are proof that paradigm collisions can stimulate creativity. New times and new challenges need not paralyze the people of God.

The Need for Continual Refocusing

Not long after founding our band of Christ-followers in Kirkland, Washington, I invited Dr. Lucky Klopp, a church consultant whom you met in chapter 2, to analyze every aspect of our church. We wanted to develop a church that had "outreach-friendly" traits. Part of the process of this consultation was to identify among the leadership any differing definitions of what a church should be.

Earlier, we had reached a decision that our church would be deliberately characterized by the following mission statements:

- We would be a church committed to carrying out church life in an environment of love, acceptance and forgiveness.
- We would be a church committed to being seeker-sensitive and outreach-focused in order to reach the unchurched in our community.
- We would be a church focused on "doing the stuff" from Monday through Friday. We would have few meetings, and much teaching and focus on the church as a force in the community.
- We would be a church focused on reaching the baby boomer culture.

Now, Dr. Klopp gathered 12 of us leaders into a focus group. We were all handed a sheet of multiple-choice questions. They ranged from "I like it best when a pastor hands out outlines with methodical Bible studies" to "I like it best when the pastor tells anecdotal stories that deal with pragmatic issues of life" and "I think a church is most successful when people are coming forward and making serious decisions to receive Christ."

These questions were designed to define attitudes regarding church life.

The following month, our consultant met with our leadership team again to review the results of the study. He and I had met earlier and we both were stunned by the diversity of perspective. I was apprehensive about how the meeting would go.

Dr. Klopp began: "Gentlemen, I have some startling news

for you. Let me list on the white board the different kinds of churches Eastside could have been. The survey you respond-ed to a month ago indicated that you each could have pre-ferred at least eight different kinds of churches."

He wrote these options on the board:

- Healing center
- Life situation teaching ministry
- Seeker-friendly church
- Pentecostal/charismatic services
- Expositional preaching center
- Sacramental church services
- Classroom/instruction church
- Hard-core evangelism/outreach church

"So, gentlemen," Dr. Klopp asked, "where do you think Eastside falls in this list?" Everyone was silent. "Which of these do you think you are?" he persisted.

When most of the leaders finally pinpointed Eastside as a seeker-sensitive congregation, I was surprised.

A few identified the church as a healing and outreach cen-ter. A lively discussion ensued. After a bit, Dr. Klopp quieted the discussion and said, "Gentlemen, let me show you what the outcome of the test was." Stepping to the chalkboard, he began to outline the spread in our definitions of what Eastside was to be.

Watching the extremes develop, one of our leaders asked, "What does this mean?"

Smiling, Dr. Klopp answered, "This means we have some problems developing around here. Most of you have been here since the beginning. You have been in planning sessions together, and yet the group still holds many antithetical defin-itions of what a church is. Can you imagine what must be hap-pening in the minds of the rest of the adherents in the church?

"I am advising Doug to develop a course immediately that will give a consistent presentation of what Eastside believes. We have a lot of strong leaders here. You are great leaders. But you must be shooting at the same target. Each of you needs to paint the same picture of what Eastside is about. You have to be looking at what you mean by "church" through the same lenses. All of you need to be on the same page, headed in the same direction."

The group chimed in their agreement.

THE MOST EFFECTIVE AMONG US WILL BE THOSE WHO CAN COMMUNICATE A VISION AND INSPIRE OTHERS TO WORK TOWARD IT.

This was a pivotal point in our congregation's history. We had found in our differences the extreme need for focus. The group's willingness to hold loosely to their own paradigms and to venture into change spoke highly of the caliber of these leaders. I was encouraged as their leader. As a group, we were committed to the deliberate development of a paradigm of what Eastside Foursquare was to be.

One of our pastors turned to me and spoke for the group: "Pastor, could you restate in your own words what we mean by 'church?'"

Confidently, I began, "The definition is the same as when we started the church. We are a church focused on reaching the baby boomer population. Our style and presentation of music is aimed at the rock culture. Our environment of ministry is devoted to a strong emphasis on love, acceptance and forgiveness. We are to be utterly and totally sensitive to those who have little or no church experience."

Reiterating the goals established at our founding offered a target and renewed our sense of focus. We had discovered our paradigm differences before we faced the cost of a full-force collision. However, we did have to find a way to make our boundaries more specific.

THE COST OF PARADIGM COLLISIONS

The failure to take paradigm collisions seriously can result in:

- Relational breakdowns;
- Wasting emotional and spiritual resources;
- Inefficient use of monetary resources;
- High levels of frustration and turnover rate among the leadership;
- High level of misunderstanding in the community at large about what the church stands for (hence, less fruitfulness).

Paradigm Paralysis

Many churches have reached the bottleneck stage of paradigm conflicts, resulting in paradigm paralysis. Not only are Christians being held to low levels of effectiveness, but the unchurched community is also having difficulty finding churches that operate under paradigms that can be easily understood. How can we move beyond a paralyzed state?

Focus on leadership. First, spend time developing the lens through which the congregation views church leadership. In my estimation, the charismatic leader who has 12 talents dripping from his fingers is not needed today. Today we need leaders who think smart and lead effectively. The most effective among us will be those who can communicate a vision and inspire others to work toward it. Particularly in the case of a church that wants to reach baby boomers, a collaborative leadership model is important to define.

Unlock people's talents. People are looking for visions that will allow them to unlock their talents and strengths. They want to be given the permission to be successful as devoted followers of Christ on His terms. It is essential that these visionary models and patterns be presented so people may launch into this paradigm enthusiastically, unleashing the power of the Spirit through their gifts.

Recognize the power of previous paradigms. The mobility of today's Christians in moving from church to church is making this issue acute. None of us leaves our spiritual roots far behind. By roots, I mean our initial experience of church life. Without deliberate paradigm analysis, most congregations are inevitably stuck or frozen in a perpetual state of paradigm collisions, unable to move ahead strategically.

I often think that all of us tend to return to our first pictures of church when we're under pressure. If a person feels pressure from having to define church as a fellowship with 5,000 members, he or she may return to the average size church of 106. If you want to change people's paradigm, you must respect it, at least to the extent of understanding it.

Statements such as, "I'm just not being fed here," or "Oh, the Holy Spirit really moved today," or "I just don't feel plugged in," are usually expressions of previously experienced paradigmatic issues, rather than value statements about the quality of the church.

"I'm Going to Get Fired"
The high cost of paradigm collisions was brought home to me after a seminar at which I shared on the topic of worship. Just

as I was about to leave, two couples caught me at the kitchen door of the hotel.

"Can we have just a minute?" asked the tallest of the four. He was about six-foot-seven, and had an authoritative presence.

I stopped and said, "Sure, how can I help?"

"Well, I think I'm going to get fired when I go home." He paused and cleared his throat. "Oh, yes—this is my wife, Naomi, my assistant, Dale, and his wife, Debbie."

He had my interest now. "Why are you getting fired?" I asked.

"Well, we wanted to reach baby boomers, so we added some chorus singing to our traditional worship services. At first it was marginally accepted, but when the elders saw we were serious about going in this direction, they called me in."

"And what was the outcome?" I had heard this scenario a few times.

"They told me that singing with a guitar wasn't up to the dignity of the gospel. They said the choruses weren't as deep as the hymns, and that they didn't feel like it was their church anymore. The leading elder said he didn't feel at home."

He was a little choked up, but continued: "I told them I wanted to develop a worshiping church, and that did it. The chairman stood up and said, 'So, you don't believe we ever worshiped the Lord before you came?'"

I listened in silence. The assistant looked at his shoes, and the women hugged each other.

Finally, I found words to speak. "Change is tough. It looks to me like you may have changed things too fast. You are obviously running into some paradigm collisions over what a church is. When your head elder said he didn't feel at home, he meant he couldn't recognize his church any longer. You may need to plant a new church at this point. At least then you'll be able to lead, rather than deal with this church's past failures."

I'm not sure what they did. I hope they didn't decide just to dangle between two paradigms of the church at worship.

THE COSTLIEST COLLISION

Churches today often don't hear the most significant paradigm collision around them because it occurs in silence. Lost people whose paradigms continually collide with traditional ways of doing church usually say nothing. Because these people aren't in church causing a fuss, church people rarely consider their view of reality or the kind of worship to which they would respond. This silent collision is the costliest of all in terms of souls that are never reached.

Avoiding collisions with those most in need of what we have to say requires investing time in discovering how these people listen. Answering questions such as these is vital:

- How do lost people in your community view the Church?
- What do they believe a pastor is?
- What do they think about the Bible?
- What do they think is most important in life?

Facts About Unchurched Listeners
Aristotle wrote about three facets of communication: the message, the messenger and the audience. Because people today hear differently than ever before, we must give special attention to the audience. As an evangelist, I have learned that one must give as much attention to the listening pattern of the audience as one does to the message. Here are some some hard and fast listening traits that today's unbelieving listeners share, in contrast to most church clientele.

They are skeptical. Today's listeners consider public leaders guilty until proven innocent. As communicators, we have to do more than accept the skepticism; we need to make it work toward making disciples by admitting that today's world consists of a great deal of sham and hypocrisy.

They don't have a concept of final authority. Today's listeners don't accept high-and-mighty pronouncements easily, especially about very personal areas in their lives. Communicators must take their listeners through a logical process and allow them to join in the process of making a conclusion. The concept of trusting an expert, church leaders or the Bible as infallible is foreign to most modern ears.

They are need-oriented listeners. Today's listeners perk up when they think their felt needs are being addressed. Of course, the believer knows that feelings are not an adequate measure of truth. However, in knowing this trait we can often lead people to their ultimate need—salvation through God's Son, Jesus Christ, and the grace and power of His indwelling Spirit.

Music communicates to them effectively. In our culture, music has become a primary conveyance of attitude, truth and vision. I was surprised recently when I noted the number of successful leaders who possess an above-average understanding and awareness of music. Seminaries would do well to focus more on contemporary styles of music if they want to produce ministers who can reach this generation.

They accentuate the positive. Some polls say Americans are very happy, while other surveys indicate that baby boomers in particular aren't "happy campers." Many of them are seeking happiness to replace the gloom within, so they will be neither attracted nor retained by appeals based on gloom, doom and fear. The churched respond fairly well to this approach, but most other people do not. It is a fact that the most positive candidates have won the last four presidential elections in America. "Tell us how good it can be" is the modern plea.

They are fiercely individualistic. Today's ears don't easily grasp concepts of community or belonging. Anything that would suggest giving up individual rights or pleasures for the benefit of the whole is beginning to sound almost "immoral." The concept of "belonging to a church" is particularly hard to communicate. Giving up rights to follow a Lord does not fit into the current patterns. Today's modern listeners barely devote themselves to their family—the basic paradigm of commitment. This all adds up to a serious soul illness from which today's seeker inevitably suffers.

Yet, research shows that these very people crave meaningful relationships. Here is an invitation to show how life in covenant with God and other believers is the most individually fulfilling life of all.

They are multisensory learners. The television generations learn best through all-sensory experiences. Gone are the days of the radio generation, when hearing alone was the dominant electronic media. Drama and music have moved from just being inspirational or entertaining to being vital ways of communicating Bible truth.

Tomorrow's audiences will be even more attuned to electronic media. Many adults are stunned by the way kids master computer programs and games that are a struggle for us. Why? They have a conceptual framework that grasps the world of the computer chip—from video games to computer golf to Word Perfect.

Recently, while playing Nintendo John Madden NFL football with my college-age son, I chuckled to myself, recalling the first football game I received for Christmas. I was probably 11 years old, and my parents bought one of those electronic games that vibrated the football players down the field. Now, here we are just a little more than 30 years later, playing at blazing speeds a game that lets you program bluffs, do audibles and pass for 50 yards. Wow!

Communicating to today's and tomorrow's listeners requires that we recognize this dramatic shift in listening and learning styles. We can't escape; the shift impacts all we do. Church just isn't going to be what it was before the year 2000. I suppose it will be better in some ways and worse in others. But different it will be.

I am determined to be a deliberate participant in tomorrow. Lord willing, I'm going to be there anyway, so I'd just as soon be working on tomorrow as allow it to work on me. Even if my brain moves at slower speeds than those who've grown up in the secular humanistic culture, I can learn to communicate with them.

DELIBERATE PARADIGM COLLISIONS

Some views of reality are worth affirming despite opposing views. One of the big issues our church regularly addresses is "loud music." Actually, this issue is probably more one of musical style rather than volume. Typically, someone from the over-60 group will say, "The music is just too loud for my friends to feel comfortable." We have learned to be philosophical rather than personal in dealing with these kinds of concerns. Our 60-plus group is a vital element of the church. Over the years, our congregation has grown to appreciate the wide spectrum of generations. We want to remain sensitive to this diversity.

Yet, we have made it clear that we have a congregational style aimed at the "rock generation." Our paradigm of church says rock is a good style for worship. Because this focus was arrived at through careful consideration, thought and prayer, it cannot be compromised. We believe that no church can be all things to all people, and we are convicted about our need to appeal to the rock generation.

This may sound like a tough stance, but it is necessary. The ability to give a forthright and clear definition of this paradigm for church helps us to address opinions to the contrary with compassion. Without a clear target group and written definitions of what churches are about, such objections become very personal. Sometimes effectiveness may call for this kind of deliberate paradigm collision.

By setting a clear picture of our aims and purposes, people are allowed to make choices. In drawing clear boundaries of how we define appropriate music for our worship, we allow ourselves the freedom to take tough positions gracefully. In turn, some decide that our paradigm isn't for them. And that's OK.

No church can be all things to all people.
Not everyone chooses the same church style.

PARADIGMS *in* PRACTICE

1. Have any recent conflicts in your church been about what your church ought to do and be? From what differing paradigms or visions of church life do they stem? What specifics do these conflicts deal with: expectations about church? the pastor? preaching? music in worship?

2. What metaphors or word pictures could you use to describe your church now? Is your church: a family? a corporation? an outreach center? a healing center, etc.? Listen for the terminologies that people use to describe your church. You may discover patterns. These patterns represent the most commonly held paradigms of what the church should be.

4

....

WHAT IS A PARADIGM SHIFT?

The Bible itself has one of the most vivid definitions of a paradigm shift. When the apostle Paul was still known as Saul and was on his way to Damascus, he was operating under a paradigm that called for him to try to stamp out the upstart Christian movement. As you recall, he was struck down suddenly with a bright light from heaven and had to be led into the city. After Ananias had laid hands on him, his sight was restored so dramatically that he could now "see" the truth about Christ and His Way—quite a drastic shift in viewpoints! The experience gave Saul a new set of lenses: Jesus Christ as Lord.

Scientist Thomas Kuhn says, "People don't begin to see new ways until they have to."[1] Crises such as that experienced by Paul on the Damascus road (see Acts 9:1-9) make us aware of our old paradigms, and virtually force a shift upon us.

This kind of disturbance in the way we've grown accustomed to viewing the world can be very disorienting. And it's become a common, if unfortunate, battleground among some church people.

A NEW PARADIGM OF MINISTRY

I sat down with Thomas, my new Mennonite friend, in the college cafeteria. I tipped my milk over while trying to get into the bench seat, but my tuna sandwich looked good. I was starved after teaching all morning.

"Man, this info is really helping me," Thomas said. "What I'm learning about baby boomers is moving me in a direction I've been thinking about for a while." He stopped long enough to slurp his coffee. I have always appreciated the intelligence and passion of any Mennonite I've met.

"How do you see yourself applying this material?" I asked. Seminar instructors all wonder if their information is ever being applied.

"Well, I'm kind of in a spot," he started. "I'm an evangelist. This is unusual for Mennonites. Do you know much about us?" he paused, waiting for my response.

Finishing my mouthful of tuna sandwich I answered, "I sure do. The Mennonite movement, like most Anabaptist groups, started off as a separatist movement. Your aim was to stay away from the world."

"You've got it. Most of us now see that we can't stay away from the world. Many of our leaders are noting that we need to reach out. We are starting new churches for folks not traditionally Mennonite. I see myself as an evangelist, but some of these new thoughts are confusing me. I see myself starting churches for those who have never gone to church," he finished enthusiastically.

"Why are you confused with your assignment?" I inquired.

"I don't have any frame of reference to which I can compare what I see happening with me. In fact, many in my heritage would be uneasy with what I want to do. But I want to be a Mennonite," he concluded as he looked up for affirmation.

"It seems like you have a great deal of support. You'll have to make a new pattern for an evangelistic church—a church for the unchurched. But it's been done before. I'm sure you will succeed. All of us today are having to develop new paradigms of ministry to match our calls and present circumstances." As I finished, the seminar attendees began to head back to their classrooms.

"Looks like I'm back to work," I concluded. We both laughed and headed off with our half-empty trays.

THE UNCHANGING RULE: PARADIGMS CHANGE

Contemporary society has been called the "post-modern" world. Even "modernism" is no longer modern. The old easy liberalism and the belief that the world is getting better every

"PROGRESS COMES THROUGH BURSTS OF REVOLUTIONARY CHANGE."—THOMAS KUHN

day in every way have fallen to the hard realities of today's chaotic social order. In the post-modern world, everything is in a process of perpetual change. Paradigms are no exception. The forces at work in the culture cause the rules to change constantly.

Differences in worldviews are a clear example of how paradigms are in flux. For example, baby busters (the children of baby boomers) don't perceive *work* as the hopeful source of satisfaction as their boomer predecessors did. Work-watchers are telling us that the average high school graduate will change jobs five times in his or her lifetime; so the world of work, as they see it, has become uncertain and unpredictable.

Revolutionary Change
Thomas Kuhn also reports, "Progress doesn't happen in a straight line. Rather, progress comes through bursts of revolutionary change."[2] Anyone who has led a church through any measure of growth has experienced what Kuhn meant.

The future holds many shocks for us. Even today, "information overload" affects the way we preach. But imagine what it will be like to communicate to a people hooked up to the fiber-optic "highway." Fiber optics is predicted to put a record number of companies out of business. Anyone with a small home studio and digital recording equipment will be able to sell tunes and worship songs through a computer modem system.

- *How will this change Christian music ministry?* Immensely, I would assume. And, with the Holy Spirit's help it will be better, I suppose.
- *How hard will people be to preach to?* Easier? Maybe. Who knows?

The Early Church also faced paradigm issues in its day that affected its theology. When Constantine legalized the Church, it was a whole new ball game. The Christian movement had to adjust from being a fellowship hiding in the catacombs of Rome, to a movement with people in high places and the Emperor on their side. No sooner had they adjusted than the Vandals from the north descended on Christian Rome. The Crusades eventually forced the question of whether converts should be made by the sword. The Enlightenment forced the Church to deal with human learning and reasoning. Sometimes our ancestors in the faith were nimble and quick of mind and spirit. At other times, they were gobbled up in the morass of change around them.

Action or Reaction?

The future will force upon us many issues that are anything but benign. Experiments such as "cryonic suspension" (being frozen after your death so you can be thawed in the future) will certainly increase. Euthanasia isn't an issue that will end when Dr. Jack Kevorkian passes on. The aging of baby boomers will be a large topic. A worldwide economy and an eventual boom will also affect the climate in which we preach.

The Church cannot afford to be sucked up in the times, but neither can we be merely reactive if we want to be effective. We have to analyze and respond deliberately to the issues and the spirit of the day. As the apostle Paul wrote, we must "test the spirits to see whether they are from God" (1 John 4:1).

DISCERNING THE SUBSTANCE

New discoveries always threaten the status quo. Hence, conflict is usually an inevitable first manifestation of change. It is essential that we discern whether the potential change is of substance or of method.

Example: The Search for the Center

Copernicus saw that the sun, rather than the earth, was the center of our solar system. In the minds of most church leaders in his time, such a perspective was a major assault on the status quo. It was widely felt that Copernicus had not just introduced another way of studying nature. He had threatened the idea that man, the main occupant of earth, was the center of God's concern. Eventually, you could be put to death for adopting Copernicus's view.

Obviously, erroneous paradigms can be destructive. But when one that is actually true confronts us, it can bear plentiful fruit. Eventually, we learned that perceiving the sun to be the center of the solar system in no way assaults the veracity of Scripture, threatens God or casts doubt on His care for people. Copernicus challenged the approach to studying astronomy, not God. Today, it is hard to imagine that the concept would bring on the loud accusation, "Heretic!"

Example: Theology and Method

Some 300 years ago, the evangelists John Wesley and George Whitefield were arguing theology. As you recall, Whitefield was one of the preachers who sparked the first "Great Awakening" in America. He was convinced that the sovereignty of God took precedence over the free will of man. On the other hand, Wesley emphasized human responsibility.

The two friends also had a falling out about method. "George," we can hear Wesley say, "you can't preach out in the open air! It's ungodly!"

"But John, I must!" Whitefield protested. "We have no buildings to meet in. Lady Huntington has promised some money, but that could take some time." We can see the blood vessels bulging in his neck.

"You can't do it, George. The church will not only object; the whole lot of us will be pegged fanatics. We can't go tearing down traditions like that. I'm going to Scotland and you'll be on your own." John calmed some as he sat down.

"The masses are hearing us, John. They won't go to the cathedrals. And the clergy know not what to do with them. You should see the response, John. They are receiving Christ by the hundreds. Don't you remember how you hungered? Besides, creation is God's cathedral," George pleaded as he also sat down.

"It may be God's creation," John replied. "But it lowers our message to the level of the common rabbler or snake-oil salesman. We are proclaimers of the Word of God. The only Word of God. I suppose you have that musician brother of yours singing with them as well. By what authority do you espouse these new preaching practices?" John's voice rose and he stood up in frustration.

"I've considered a number of factors, John. *Anything not directly forbidden by the Scriptures is free to be done.* Anything encouraged must be done by whatever means. We are commanded to preach the gospel as Christ did. And He did it in the open. If the means don't compromise the central message and if they attract the attention of those who've not heard before, it must be done!" George remained seated.

John wasn't finished. "Our preachers in England are following your example. Why, every street corner in England will be a chapel at the rate you're going. We'll all be laughing stocks of England, George!" John's voice peaked an octave as he finished.

"Sorry you feel that way, John. If we fail to bring the gospel to the people, our own nation will go the way of France!" George said with the staccato of a man finished with a topic— which was his way.

John stood up. "You speak persuasively. I will become more vile myself to reach those locked outside the blessing of the gospel."

What amazing flexibility on Wesley's part! He was able to see that if their differing emphases over Calvinism and Arminianism did not divide them, then mere method must not be allowed to either.

What Business Are We In?
Business and management consultant Tom Peters illustrated what happens when we refuse to make paradigm shifts, in a

videotape titled *The Search for Excellence*. He pointed out that the train industry missed its grand opportunity to own the discovery of the automobile. Railroad industry leaders did not seize on the automotive revolution for the simple reason that they didn't understand the business they were in. In Peters' words, "They thought that they were in the train business. But, they were in fact in the *transportation* business. Time passed them by, as did opportunity. They couldn't see what their real purpose was."[3]

How often is this happening to our churches? Often!

Let me pose a question: Are we in the hymn-singing business or the worshiping business?

What paradigm could you be holding onto too tightly, wrongly feeling that change threatens substance instead of method? Could you be missing the opportunity for greater effectiveness? Could it be that methods that once worked are now your greatest obstacle? These essential questions are at the heart of paradigm shifts.

Changers or Victims?

Our societal change quotient has risen to hyper levels. Do our churches show an interest in keeping up? Do our paradigms match present challenges and new opportunities? For the most part, no.

Becoming Changers

However, a rising tide of awareness is emerging today. We are beginning to admit that new times require new methodologies. These methodologies require new paradigms to establish boundaries of what a successful church looks like.

Typically, a few leaders—paradigm pioneers—will understand that crisis is a friend. So some will become deliberate paradigm-shapers who change the world. Without deliberate change, we will succumb to the change triggered by crisis.

As I shared with you, this happened in the first church I attended. All of us longhaired, patchouli-soaked kids changed that church forever. What was the issue? Not whether the church was the Body of Christ, but whether kids with long hair should be allowed to change the nature of the church's outreach. As it turned out, a few of the older members accepted the new paradigm. Although they would never have invited the crisis that prompted them to change, they adjusted their lenses enough to allow their leaders to be agents of change.

Becoming a Victim

Unfortunately, the older attenders of this church became victims. They could have helped to shape the new paradigm. It is always better to get a jump on change around you. The church is too often victimized.

That's how I felt some years ago when I was the leader of a small Bible college. We'd had some sexual misconduct during the school year, and I reacted strongly against an article in *Campus Life* magazine, I felt it was too accepting of physical contact, so I wrote them a hot letter informing them that I'd never advertise in their magazine again. (A move that would definitely hurt us more than it would *Campus Life*.)

I believe it was Philip Yancey who wrote back a great letter. It read something like this:

> Dear Doug,
>   Sorry about your response. Our mission is to help kids on campus. I think you'll find that we have carefully researched the issues they are facing. We are attempting to meet them where they are. We are seeking to understand before being understood. We stand by our approach.

Our mission is different from yours. We respect
yours, but the culture we are addressing sets the
need for us to speak the way we do.

Cordially,
Campus Life

Now, nearly 20 years later, I feel like a fool. Although I have
no regrets about the substance of my stand in behalf of biblical morality, my ability to reach the culture I wanted to win

THE INESCAPABLE REALITY IS: CHANGE OR YOU'LL BE CHANGED.

was threatened by my reactionary, victim-like response.

The inescapable reality is: Change or you'll *be* changed.
Campus Life understood this. Without compromising doctrine
or values, they were communicating in the milieu of their listeners—and they continue to do so.

THE MINISTRY OF CARING

New problems require new solutions. New solutions usually
force paradigm shifts. This fact of life has become especially
evident in the ministry of pastoral care.

Most churches have certain frameworks or types of ministry
they fall into almost automatically when they deal with human
problems. For example, some emotionally distraught people
in one church might be told that they need deliverance from

demonic oppression. The same persons might be encouraged in another church to see a family counselor, or to attend a 12-step group. In yet another setting they might be encouraged to see someone who can prescribe psycho-pharmaceutical drugs to heal their emotional strain. Another might suggest a certain amount of Bible memorization, and still another may offer a combination of the above. How groups address such issues is determined by their paradigms.

Remember that we are rarely moved to another paradigm without a crisis. If someone memorizes 20 verses and is still depressed, we might consider that enough of a crisis to reexamine our paradigm of caring for that person.

If we refuse to consider a paradigm shift, we should ask whether this refusal is based on faith or fear. The refusal to change is often based on our fear that the realities we have held as true in the past might be taken from us. However, such an experience might also open us up to a broader understanding of healing. This crisis could change our paradigm of how we do ministry. A positive paradigm shift always results in greater insight.

CHALLENGING SHIFTS BEFORE US

I believe the contemporary Church faces several new challenges to old paradigms in our day. Lest we think this is something new, let's remember this has always been the case. As we have said, one of life's certainties is that life certainly changes.

Also to the Greek
Acts 10 illustrates a dramatic paradigm shift in Paul and Peter's day. Until Peter's vision of clean and unclean animals, and his encounter with the Gentile Cornelius, the Church was thought

of as an exclusively Jewish sect, a subgroup in Judaism. But in telling Peter not to call anything impure that He had made clean, God gave the Church a chance to make a deliberate shift to become a church for all races. There ensued no small shaking in the Jewish church in Jerusalem.

Although the Jerusalem council sent word that the Gentiles were not to be required to become full observants of the Law,

IT'S IMPOSSIBLE TO MAKE A PARADIGM SHIFT WORK IN BEHALF OF THE KINGDOM WITHOUT REMEMBERING THE VISION. IT'S IMPOSSIBLE TO HOLD TO A NEW PARADIGM WITHOUT COMMITMENT.

the elders at Jerusalem apparently made little effort to apply the same principle to Gentiles there. Instead, the center of the mighty missionary movement in the Early Church shifted to Antioch of Syria.

What would have happened if the church in Jerusalem had dared to make this paradigm shift? How would church history have read if it had responded to this crisis with a strategy that involved more than just allowing Paul and his team to enact a mission to the Greeks?

New challenges such as this require deliberate paradigm shifts. In turn, deliberately directing such a shift requires:

- Seeing in a crisis more opportunities than problems.
- Recognizing the difference between substance and method, underlying values and technique.
- Thinking "win/win" instead of "win/lose."

The Call to Commitment

Once a paradigm shift is affirmed, a great deal of courage is required to stick to the new direction. The apostle Peter was privileged to be in on the ground floor of the mission to the Gentiles because of his vision and the encounter with Cornelius. But it was Paul who wound up really championing the paradigm shift. Peter apparently tried to have it both ways—allowing the gospel to be preached to the Gentiles, but holding on to traditional Jewish prejudice in public. He was trying to live between two paradigms, and Paul had to boldly challenge him on this point (see Gal. 2:11-21).

I can imagine Paul saying: "Come on, Pete, get with the program! This is our future—reaching Gentiles. Don't you remember the vision?"

It's impossible to make a paradigm shift work in behalf of the Kingdom without remembering the vision. It's impossible to hold to a new paradigm without commitment.

Shifts That Call to Us

Is the Church today running the risk of being victimized by our own old paradigms, as was the church in Jerusalem? I think so. Let me list a few danger areas I have observed as a practitioner.

The failure to reach baby boomers. As a whole, the modern Church underestimates the difference between the Truman generation and baby boomers. I hear some talk about reaching boomers, but those who are courageous enough to deliberately direct a paradigm shift aren't nearly as numerous as those who like to talk about it.

Neglecting the small-group movement. Small groups are essential for fellowship and intimacy, especially in large churches. Yet, recent studies have shown that small-group attendance is declining. Will we just stand by idly and watch them die?

The needs of "the church-inexperienced." Thousands of

people think and speak seriously about life and death, moral failure, relationships—many of the very topics we talk about in church—but we refuse to package our message in a way that invites them to join the conversation.

Today's new family. Despite the fact that the two-parent, 2.3-child family has been so widely replaced by singles, single-parent, no-children and blended-marriage families, many churches refuse to make a paradigm shift that allows them to minister to such families effectively.

Dysfunctional and depressive disorders. Anywhere from 20 to 33 percent of the people in the United States will experience a major episode of depression during their lifetime. Yet, depression is one of the major reasons people seek Christ. But our view of depressive disorders is often so simplistic we cannot meet such people at their point of need.

ANOTHER SHIFT BEFORE US

"Let's start a buster service," said Robert (names are changed) in our planning session.

"We can try," Mike offered, "but I know there's already something we can do to assimilate this twenty-something group."

We were discussing one of our major concerns: How we, as a boomer church, could reach the boomer children—the busters. We were concerned that we deliberately try to set a pattern for ministry that said to busters loud and clear: We take you very seriously!

I spoke up. "I've never felt it was right to say to any one group, 'You're the church of tomorrow.' They really are the church of today. But I know we need to reach the boomers."

"Actually, we're reaching twenty-something people just fine," Mike interrupted me.

"Well," I said, "from my searching and reading, and from

my visiting other settings, I've concluded two things. One, in terms of music, our services are very compatible for busters. We could add a little volume now and then and it won't bother boomers.

"Two, the real deal is that busters don't like seeing just boomers up front." I paused for a breath. "So, I don't think any of us can do the meeting." I stopped and smiled.

"I think you're right," Robert said, "but what are we going to do?" He looked at Mike.

"I think we should do the best we can with boomers, include more busters in our services and have 'busters only' small groups," Mike submitted.

"You're right," I agreed. "I don't think we'll be as effective as a church that focuses on busters. But it's not like trying to keep the Truman generation and the boomers together. And I think Mike is right. We'd better prayerfully recruit leaders for a twenty-something group." I paused with the realization that a thought had just hit me.

"I tell you, we're going to have to change or we'll miss a very special opportunity. It's going to be a bit uncomfortable—as it was for the men years ago when we added women to the church council—but I see no choice. In the meantime, we need to plan for the day when we have a special service for this age group. I think younger busters are going to be adaptable to our style." I left the subject open for further discussion.

Our plan was set. It felt right. It sounded right. But I knew it wasn't going to *feel* right the first time a 20-year-old led worship in our predominantly thirty- and forty-something age crowd.

THE PAINFUL PROCESS OF CHANGE

Change is a painful process. Working out new patterns in the fabric of our lives can be painful. The slightest change feels very radical when experienced. Most people like to think they're change-friendly, but most people aren't.

My experience with the pain of change has been the same as reported by Arnold Mitchell in his book *Nine American Lifestyles.*[4] In the chapter entitled "The Mechanics of Change," the following pattern effectively describes the change process as experienced in the Church.

Step 1: Change Stems from Dissatisfaction
The effective change process begins with dissatisfaction. Those people who receive Christ at a high point of dissatisfaction in their lives are those who make lifetime commitments. Recall again the long-term commitment—to the point of death—of the apostle Paul after his Damascus road crisis.

When a church is deeply dissatisfied with the effectiveness of its problem-solving methods, it is a candidate for new insights. Just as people usually look for new solutions when they are highly dissatisfied with their lives, so churches and other groups grow through dissatisfaction. As cultures shift, and change comes from within and without, existing patterns of behavior are threatened. Hence, we are driven on our search. How can we be more effective? How can we be more satisfied with what we are dealing with? How can we deal with apparently unsolvable new problems? Paradigm pioneers see crisis as the threshold to new discoveries.

The emotionally mature person—and church—understands that disappointment and dissatisfaction are gifts from the Holy Spirit to lead us to greater heights. Dissatisfaction is the catalyst for change.

Step 2: Change Takes Energy
Change takes a terrific amount of emotional and physical energy. This may be why most change is associated with youth. The energy to change isn't often present in established churches.

This is why new blood will usually precede change in a church.

In 2 Corinthians 3, the apostle Paul spoke of the Christian life as a lifestyle of transformation. We "are *changed* into the same image from glory to glory" (v. 18, *KJV*, italics added). A change-friendly environment characterizes God's presence.

Groups who change effectively find the energy to implement new ideas. Individuals rarely change their lives without an energy resource that is adequate for the change required. As every pastor knows, some people broken by addiction or bound by the memory of painful events don't have the emotional reserves to face much change in their lives.

Step 3: Change Requires Insight
Arnold Mitchell sees the insight to know what changes will work as an essential key to group change. Insight must be present through all of the change process. The absence of credible know-how to move on to the next step can freeze the change process. But with insightful leadership, the new paradigms can become the "Eureka!" experience in the change process.

Visionary paradigm pioneers "sell" groups they lead on how easily change can occur. Groups with dissatisfaction need a leader who can show them how to make a paradigm leap.

PITFALLS IN THE PROCESS

To summarize, the process of change requires:

DISSATISFACTION
ENERGY   INSIGHT

Sometimes a church will have one or more of these elements, but not all. We must beware of at least three pitfalls that face us if all these elements aren't present.

Pitfall 1

Dissatisfied groups that have a lot of energy, but no insight, tend to run around in all directions and accomplish nothing. They also chew up their leaders and one another emotionally.

Pitfall 2

Groups who are dissatisfied with insight but have no energy to change, simply sit around and complain.

Pitfall 3

Some groups have insight and energy but aren't dissatisfied enough to do anything about it. These are groups or leaders who maintain the status quo but are never active changers.

ENJOYING THE PROCESS

Despite the pain change can bring, and despite the pitfalls before us, effective paradigm pioneers enjoy the excitement of the paradigm shift. They know that change can occur when the Spirit indwells them and enables them to combine the ingredients of the change process skillfully. They know their work is cut out for them, recognizing that others often *don't* enjoy the change process. On the other hand, they have sized up their "balcony people," and they count on others who share the vision to cheer on the process.

Eventually, the new ideas are adapted by the Church at large. The new paradigms then become business as usual. We have seen a handful of such movements in the Church. One of the mightiest paradigm shifts was the Reformation. At the turn of the century, and again in the '60s, there was the charismatic/Pentecostal renewal. The experience of Calvary Chapel and the Jesus People, once viewed as radical, is now viewed as normative in many circles and is emulated instead of criticized. These are all instances of new paradigms for solving problems being embraced by the Church at large.

We can be assured that tomorrow will bring problems that cannot be solved by today's insights. But this is exciting to real directors of paradigm shifts. This is the realm in which the Holy Spirit dwells. This is the realm in which true leaders thrive.

Paradigm pioneers are always those who are willing to fail, to stick their necks out for what they believe. They may be wrong much of the time, but they are right often enough to achieve things that the fearful cannot even dream of.

THE OLD APPLE TREE

James Michener shared the following story that inspires me to embrace shifts in my own life:

> We must go back nearly eighty years to when I was a country lad. The farmer at the end of our lane had an apple tree which had once produced fruit, but now had lost its energy to give us apples. The farmer, on an early spring day I still remember, found eight nails, long and rusty, which he hammered into the trunk of the reluctant tree. Four were knocked in close to the ground, on different sides of the trunk; four higher and again well dispersed around the circumference.
>
> That autumn a miracle happened. The tired old tree had been goaded back to life, and produced a bumper crop of red, juicy apples, bigger and better than we had seen before. When I asked how this happened, the farmer explained:
>
> "Hammerin' in the rusty nails gave it a shock to

remind it that its job is to produce apples."

I asked, "Was it important that the nails were rusty?"

He responded, "Maybe it made the mineral in the nail easier to digest."

My next question was, "Was eight important?"

"If you are going to send a message, be sure that it is heard."

"Could you do the same next year?"

"A substantial jolt lasts about ten years."

"Will you knock in more nails?"

"By that time we both may be finished," he said.

But I was unable to verify this prediction. For by that time our family had moved away from the lane.[5]

Creating the hunger for change—driving in the nails—is an essential aspect of deliberate paradigm leaders. Teaching a group to use the jolt positively in a process of meaningful change is another.

Change is inevitable.

Change is desirable.

Change is exhilarating.

PARADIGMS *in* PRACTICE

1. How would you rate the dissatisfaction level in your life and in your congregation regarding your *fruitfulness?* Is it enough to have a will for change?

2. Are there problems with present practices, assumptions and methods that you are finding unresolvable? If so, look again at the requirements for change—dissatisfaction, energy

and insight—and ask whether one or more of these elements are missing in your situation.

3. Do you see yourself as an inspirational leader who can develop the desire and energy to face the challenge of change? If not, maybe some reading in the following resources could provide mentoring along this path.

Notes

1. Thomas S. Kuhn, *The Structure of Scientific Revolutions* (Chicago: University of Chicago Press, 1962), pp. 66-91.
2. Ibid., p. 160.
3. Tom Peters, *In Search of Excellence* (video) (San Francisco: HarperCollins-Warner Books, 1982).
4. Arnold Mitchell, *Nine American Lifestyles* (New York: Warner Books, 1983).
5. James A. Michener, *The Eagle and the Raven* (New York: Tom Doherty Publications, 1990), pp. 3-6.

5

....

CHANGE-FRIENDLY CHURCHES

Do not pray for easy lives! Pray to be stronger men.
Do not pray for tasks equal to your powers. Pray for
powers equal to your tasks. Then the doing of your
work shall be no miracle, but you shall be a miracle.
—Phillip Brooks[1]

If you're the leader of a church that is friendly to change, you may well feel that your work *is* a miracle after all. Too often, paradigm shifts are hard to communicate. But when there is a communications breakthrough—when the church as a whole begins to accept the idea that the only unchanging fact of life is change—the whole atmosphere becomes user-friendly to those whose needs the change was designed to meet.

One reason churches would do well to become change-friendly is that paradigm shifts often occur undetected. For example, at one time Japanese products were considered to be cheap and defective. But the marketplace paradigm changed. Soon, to speak of a Toyota was to speak of excellence. Like shifts in the marketplace, such changes occurred while we slept. Undetected or not, however, it was a radical change. The Church must grow in flexibility to be able to act on such quiet, but comprehensive, paradigm shifts.

SEASONS OF CHANGE

It is essential that church leaders understand the common experience of change. Paradigm shifts are unavoidable at three vital times in the life of a local church. It is essential to understand the nature of these periods.

Numerical Growth
Numerical growth brings an enforced introduction to change. Unless your church never exceeds the 100-member barrier, you will see shifts in perspective as new members are added. We could argue whether a larger church is of higher quality than a small one, but that isn't the issue here. I am certain that quality can exist in any size church. But significant growth does force change in a church's definition of itself.

Some thresholds of numerical change are like changing from 6-man to 11-man football. Others are more like switching from football to basketball. Initial enthusiasm may be followed by an unexpected drop in morale.

Services once held only at 11:00 A.M. may now be held at 8:30 A.M., 10:30 A.M. and 1:00 P.M. Being unable to anticipate which service one's friends will attend can cause a paradigm collision.

As churches change from, say, a facility that seats 400 to one that seats 4,000, the shifts are immense. As the church moves through the 400 threshold, additional pastors are required. The self-identity of the church changes.

The way a church views its pastor in the church of 100 people is radically different from that in a church of 600. And no wonder—the way a leader acts must change radically. Choosing for which of its pastors to provide a home may be perplexing to those who hold to a single-pastor paradigm.

A Changing Community

A second occasion when a church will face change is when the community is undergoing change. This is especially common in medium- or large-size cities. Our community, for example, is highly populated with baby boomers. As we move into the next millennium, we are anticipating that our populace will be much older. We are working on scenarios that would define what an elderly baby boomer church looks like. It isn't likely that the boomers will become duplicates of their older parents. It is more likely that they will remain a "rock" generation into their octogenarian years.

We suspect that these baby boomers may move farther out to the suburbs or into the city, leaving our area to younger renters. I am already observing changes in the immediate vicinity of our church as renters replace homeowners around our facility.

Ethnic changes especially affect a community, and may cause a church to become an anachronism. A church that is predominantly white in an area that now is populated by a broader ethnicity may not have much hope of effectiveness.

New paradigms of a church ought to be flexible enough to match the church's new context. The need for a shift may occur several times in the life of a church. Leaders ought to have contingency plans for how they will meet major shifts in the communities by having new paradigms of "doing church."

Some shifts occur slowly, like the proverbial "frog in the kettle." You remember the experiment in which the temperature of the kettle is turned up so gradually the frog never notices, until he is cooked. I have observed a subtle shift because of the scandals of PTL and Jimmy Swaggart. I have also noted that our community has slowly changed its reaction to leadership over the last few years. Such subtle changes from without the church must be faced with alert realism.

Effective church strategies are influenced by perceptions of the community at large. We have had to fit into a very specific niche and use paradigms that are consistent with our mission in expressing our identity to our community.

New Opportunities for Ministry

The third time a church will face the need for a paradigm shift is when new opportunities for meeting needs present themselves. For example, as a community ages, a church that has focused on reaching baby boomers may find itself needing to reach their children, baby busters.

These challenges become especially critical if a church is not consciously change-friendly. A hard-won self-identity can actually keep the group from seizing new opportunities. Boundaries of success—the target audiences we've learned to reach—may be so restrictive that we are not open to methods that reach other kinds of people.

When churches begin to see that their self-identity is not allowing them to seize opportunities, it is time to investigate deliberate paradigm shifts. If we don't take such measures, change may be forced upon us negatively.

The apostle Paul said, "When I was a child, I talked like a child....[but] When I became a man, I put childish ways behind me" (1 Cor. 13:11). Similarly, it is a fact of church life that ministry programs can have limited periods of effectiveness, and must also be put behind us. Many churches have too many cadavers of ministries that were once effective but are now lying around draining resources.

Twelve-step group ministries, for example, could run their

course within the decade. Although baby boomers, typically, have a high incidence of addiction, it is unlikely that this will continue at the present rate as they age. Churches who use 12-step programs as the basis for their ministry may find themselves out of step in a few years. We must ask questions such as, Are the dynamics that work in a family addicted in their 30s still at work when they reach their late 40s and 50s? The answers to such questions may require entirely different ministries. If ministry is to succeed, we must hold loosely to today's methods and try to anticipate tomorrow's challenges.

STRUGGLES IN CHANGING

Struggles with achieving consensus in the midst of the need to make paradigm changes are the ragged edges of paradigm frontiers. But if the struggle does not occur, the result will be missed opportunities for ministry.

Back to the Future?

The first step when difficulties are encountered in making a paradigm shift is to look at the church's self-definition. Once that issue is clarified, the group may be ready to move into its new future.

At Eastside, we were having great difficulty in shifting the congregation from a megachurch to a *meta*church format. The Greek pronoun *meta* means "with." A metachurch is a church of people who stand *with* each other and offer support to each other, instead of passively receiving help from professionals.

Our congregation was not established with a focus on the small groups in which such care from fellow Christians is best ministered. I highly regret this. Churches based on small groups will be far more effective in tomorrow's world.

But as the needs of our target audiences changed, our leaders became enthused about a model of church life that put responsibility for mutual caring in the hands of small groups. We very quickly realized that just choosing small-group leaders and scheduling meetings would not allow us to reach our aim. We had to go all the way back to deal with our paradigm of what a church was.

A Conflict in Paradigms

For one thing, many people had been in home groups that were heavy-handed. Their past experiences did not fit our model of small groups based on love, acceptance and forgiveness. As a consequence, many people resisted becoming a part of the small-group ministry.

Furthermore, most of our congregation had a model of care that required paid professionals to do most of the pastoral ministry, having only occasional assistance from lay leaders. And many on our staff had been trained in "doing" ministry, rather than "facilitating" ministry in groups. It took us a year of repeated discussion and training to understand the difference. Then the entire staff, including myself, had to go through the painful process of responding deliberately rather than instinctively.

Finally, many responded as though the small groups were another program to be added to the existing ministries. They did not realize that *all* of our programs would be organized on a small-group model that emphasized the work of laypeople.

I remember one conversation in particular:

"I perceive that this place is in constant turmoil," said Sam, one of our leaders, after a Wednesday night service. "Don't you think people require stability?"

"Yes," I admitted. "I've probably changed too many things in the past, and perceptually it hurts now. But the discussion I had tonight about laypeople doing 80 percent of the care is causing necessary turmoil." I like Sam. I'd felt comfortable with his evaluations in the past.

"I can see what you are saying. You know, I think you might want to step back and deal with identity. Who are we as a church? This need-approach has left some of us a little confused. I see what you're getting at, but some need to be assured that we are still Eastside." Sam patted me on the shoulder and turned to talk to friends.

OFTEN GROWTH SIMPLY CAN'T OCCUR WITHOUT PAIN. NEW WAYS OF THINKING DO NOT EMERGE WITHOUT STRESS.

I continued to pray and talk with people, but filed his comments away in the back of my mind.

So what did we do?

I produced two tapes on Eastside's philosophy of ministry. Then we produced videos illustrating how care could be administered to each other, and showed them in our services. And we established a system of accountability that made certain all leaders deployed volunteers.

We started a course called "Church 101" that describes how a lay-driven church looks compared to a professionally driven church.

We also established a sermon schedule that allowed two other people besides myself to present messages on our mission and philosophy as a church. We also began celebrating and honoring our lay leaders in the services.

We required all our primary leaders to work through a set of tapes and readings. Once a quarter, I met with our vital leaders—on a Sunday morning—to emphasize the importance of these meetings. Someone else preached the message in the auditorium while we met.

Such rigorous steps in paradigm shaping helps to present a clear congregational identity. It accelerates our journey toward what we believe are God's aims for us.

Positive Pain

We concluded the last chapter with an exercise that called for you to identify the greatest obstacles to your aims. We encouraged you to sample areas of dissatisfaction in your ministry group. This exercise was designed to develop sensitivity to dissatisfaction.

We know the truth in the expression "growing pains." Often growth simply can't occur without pain. New ways of thinking do not emerge without stress. As we have learned, dissatisfaction and crisis are the breeding grounds for new discoveries. In his book *Future Edge,* Joel Barker asserts, "One ought to locate the greatest problems and crisis because it is at this point will come the greatest new discoveries."[2]

A Dubious Skill

Too often church leaders become masters at problem avoidance. This skill inhibits growth! Crises and problems are the best soil for growing churches. They are evidence of the Holy Spirit's work. There will never be a time when we will not have problems. They are to be embraced, not avoided. Every crisis could contain the key to your congregation's self-discovery.

The apostle Paul's most intense set of problems was with the church in Corinth. His first letter is filled with rebuke and correction. If the leaders at Corinth had smoothed over the situation to avoid conflict, no positive change could have occurred. But the pressure Paul placed on them was taken seriously. And he could finally write:

> I see that my letter hurt you, but only for a little while. See what this godly sorrow has produced in you: what earnestness, what eagerness to clear yourselves, what indignation, what alarm, what longing, what concern, what readiness to see justice done. At every point you have proved yourselves to be innocent in this matter. By all this we are encouraged (2 Cor. 7:8,11,13).

We are preparing to do "exit interviews" with people who have ceased attending our church. Essentially, we are asking them a simple question, Why did you leave?

From an emotional standpoint, I am not particularly looking forward to reading the responses. As a leader, however, I am anticipating how we can better serve those we seek to love. I also am anticipating that we will probably have to reexamine our skill at communicating paradigms. We are likely to discover we've done a great job at fulfilling the aims of our paradigms, but that we did not adequately explain them to those who have different paradigms, and they moved on.

The Vindication of Strain
Paradigm strain exists when our present self-definition or paradigms don't fit or answer the present problem. New problems and opportunities require new answers and new approaches. Despite the strain this brings, we can be encouraged by the fact that the history of the Church is filled with positive outcomes of such paradigm strain.

Paradigm strain can occur when such issues as AIDS thrust themselves upon a church. They occur when a new audience is targeted—as when a church shifts from focusing on baby boomers to baby busters. The busters' love of a high energy environment and loud music, and their desire to be led by their peers, can put off older people.

Yet, if we can manage the shifts while enduring the strain, the struggle to turn such corners will be vindicated. Earlier, I mentioned that the "Jesus People" movement was considered a radical step for the Church in the '70s. Yet, today the aspects of this movement are owned by the Church at large. The new has merged into the old. The old embraced the new and the whole was changed. This pattern will continue in the future. If a new method is of God, the strain of the paradigm shift it requires will be forgotten in the realization that God has used it for His glory.

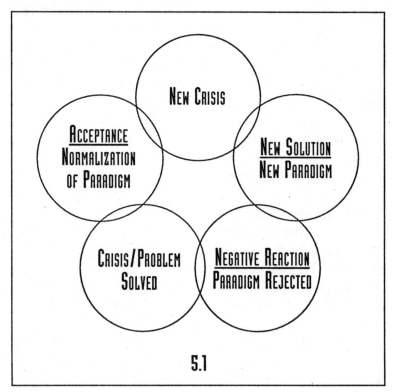

5.1

Paradigm-Sensitive Leadership

Just waking up one day and arbitrarily changing the game is very disconcerting to a group. It is important to take some time in advance of these changes to prepare both followers and midlevel leaders. This is what I mean by "paradigm-sensitive leadership."

Three distinct stages of growth are: a new problem or crisis, paradigm strain and new paradigm experimentation.

Sensitive Self-Definition

One of the reasons Eastside has been able to successfully traverse many growth thresholds is that we have focused on our self-definition. We are constantly having to define the rules of the game we are playing before we start the game. The players need to know by which rules they are living.

Many of our leaders began to question whether we wanted to reach out beyond baby boomers, primarily because at that time no one was reaching them. So we did a values check. At the core, however, our self-definition told us that we were committed to outreach. So when other churches began to reach boomers, and when their children, the busters, came into view, we were able to negotiate a shift in ministry and method.

Sensitivity to Stages of Growth
Church leaders must be aware of three distinct stages of growth:

- New problem or crisis;
- Paradigm strain;
- New paradigm experimentation.

Experimentation: Is It Necessary?
Being a sensitive leader does not mean bowing to the resistance some people have against experimentation. Theorists can stay home when the paradigm shifts start. Successfully negotiating a paradigm shift calls for adventurers who are comfortable with experimentation.

When we set out at Eastside to reach baby busters, we immediately experienced the strain of experimentation. It was a shock to admit that our boomer culture was not necessarily God's culture. How did we settle this? We began to experiment with being a multigenerational church.

Note that for nearly a decade and a half we had been a baby boomer church. Now we sought to add a dimension that was buster-friendly. The values statements of Eastside Church are strong enough to stretch out into a new generation. But this paradigm strain caused us to ask whether it is worth the pain to experiment with being multigenerational. We believe that the answer is yes.

For some reason, Christian movements tend to attract highly conservative people. Maybe our overconservatism has not allowed us to attract the most innovative of our society. But times are changing. Entrepreneurial types are beginning to move into the Church. The challenges of tomorrow will necessitate leaders who are unafraid to experiment, while able to present its rationale with sensitivity.

Of course, not all experiments work. We began our baby buster service at 2:00 P.M. on Sunday. Then we held it on

Friday night. Now we have switched to events following our Saturday night service, and have decided to include busters in the main services as leaders. I suspect we have more experimentation to do.

Being careful to teach people about the change cycle in the journey of our church is essential in winning their confidence when proposing changes and monetary investment. As our work progresses, the pattern of change broadens:

- New paradigm crisis or problem;
- Paradigm strain;
- New paradigm experimentation—rejection;
- Successful solution;
- Acceptance.

Now our church has embraced our efforts. The key to our success will be embracing the experimentation. We have allocated a significant budgeting of energy to this task. Someday when the cycle is complete we should look not young and inventive, but normal:

- New paradigm crisis or problem;
- Paradigm strain;
- New paradigm experimentation—rejection;
- Successful solution;
- Acceptance;
- Paradigm is normative.

In the future, churches will discover many different kinds of services. Within my lifetime, I fully expect to have church every day of the week. The paradigm of multiple kinds of services will be normative. We are working, for example, to present in story form and word pictures descriptions of what we mean by a multigenerational church, a church that has multistyles, but is still committed to central values. We are becoming far more than a baby boomer church, but as we change we must be careful to bring the people along through new paradigms.

I would encourage you to share this process with your leaders. This could allow them to understand that change is friendly and that it can be successfully commandeered.

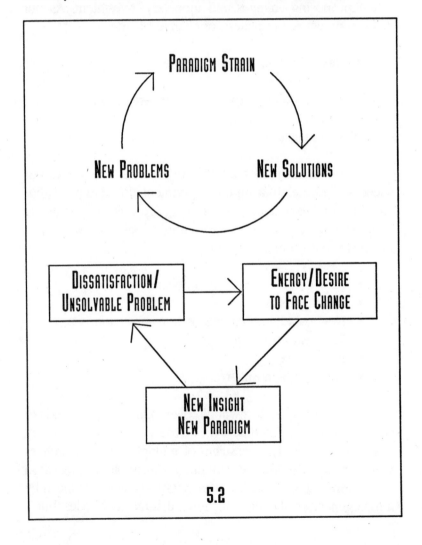

5.2

Changing While Staying the Same

Laypeople really don't want to be obstacles to growth. They want to be accessed as growth agents. The problem is, we understand so little about how change works in the church, we don't know how to keep up with it. Often our leaders are left in confusion as well. Communicating the limitations and extent of change can help allay both confusion and resistance.

Some time ago, an elderly gentleman approached me after one of our services. He said, "You aren't doing anything so new. You are saying all the old stuff, except you are saying it in a new way."

"That's exactly what we are trying to do," I said.

"I thought that this was a totally new way, but it is the same old thing stated in a new way."

My response was simple, "The way we are doing things will always be in flux. Our message never changes, because our message is the unchangeable King of the unshakable Kingdom, the Lord Jesus Christ."

He caught the picture. He felt convinced that our basic values would not change, but that we would be free to make paradigm shifts at the level of methods and means.

REVIEWING THE PROCESS

Let's look again at the stages of paradigm change that are necessary for a church to be change-friendly. They consist of:

- A change in the lenses through which a church views the real world, as well as itself;
- A change in the boundaries and definitions of success;
- A change—possibly a radical change—in the rules of the game or how the church will accomplish its mission.

Reviewing the times or seasons of change, we can recall that paradigm shifts are most likely to confront a congregation:

- When numerical growth occurs;
- When societal/cultural/economic forces change;
- When new opportunities for ministry present themselves.

"How Do You Do It?"

Does it matter whether we keep these points in mind? I once experienced an affirmation of their importance.

My unchurched friend asked me, "How many services did you do on Christmas this year?"

"We did five, and they were all nearly full," I answered.

"How many people came?" he inquired further.

"About 5,000 people," I answered.

"Man, how do you get so many people to come? I've got to check this out," he said with a genuine tone of interest.

"Well, I try to understand our community, attitudinally as well as spiritually. We have developed a view of church that is both for those who just want to kick the tires, and for those who desire to make a radical commitment to what we are talking about," I said, hoping for another question.

"What is our community attitude?" he said, after a contemplative pause.

"Well, I know that most people in our community value their time, so I keep things fast-paced and don't waste much time. And I know most people are skeptical about me—I accept that, and expect to have to win their trust, which means I don't boss everyone around.

"I know we are a community that appreciates excellence, so I kill myself on my messages. And we make certain our music and videos and dramas are as good as possible." I stopped to catch my breath. I was pretty charged up that my friend had finally expressed some interest in Eastside.

"Videos? Man! Church sounds a lot different from when I was a kid," he commented.

"Oh yeah! I forgot to say that we believe people learn and grow through multisensory input, so we use all forms of communication just as any group striving for excellence would," I added, as I turned to leave.

"Hey, I might see you next week," he said, following me out. "It sounds like you have a really different way of thinking about yourselves. I like it."

We shook hands and went our separate ways.

But I left with reason to hope our paths might someday unite. People are surprised when we take them into consideration in planning our definitions of church.

PARADIGMS in PRACTICE

1. Make two lists—one of your current ministries, and the other of current needs you see in your community. Do they match?

2. Think ahead to the next decade. What changes in felt needs can you project? How will your paradigm for ministry need to shift to meet these changing needs?

3. Are there instances in your recent church life when you were unable to seize a ministry opportunity because the self-identity of the church resisted going outside of its established boundaries or paradigms?

4. Suppose your ministry opportunity is to develop a 12-step program for various addictions. Is there fear among your church members of having addicts among them?

Notes

1. Mrs. Charles E. Cowan, *Streams in the Desert No. 1* (Grand Rapids, MI: Cowan Publications, Div. of Zondervan Publishing Co., 1965), p. 243.
2. Joel Arthur Barker, *Future Edge: Discovering New Paradigms of Success* (New York: William Morrow and Company, 1992), p. 44.

6

....

CONTEMPLATING CHANGE

A recent article in *U. S. News and World Report* stated that Wang
Laboratories lost its position of leadership in the computer
world because of its failure to keep pace with innovations, on
which this fast-changing industry depends. Wang, the article
said, lost the very skill at anticipating change that it once stood
for. And it cost the company its place in the market.[1]

Imagination and innovation can mean the difference
between success and failure in the Church no less than in the
business world. Einstein said that imagination is more important than intelligence. The gift of imagination is a powerful
tool of the Holy Spirit. Innovators skillfully use word pictures
to etch on others' hearts their dreams of what could be.

An Outmoded Paradigm

Innovation must be an ongoing process, not limited to a burst
of creativity. Let me illustrate by describing another crisis our
church faced a few years ago.

The Megachurch Problem

Eastside had always been a very outreach-centered church. We had strongly referred to ourselves as a "bringing and including" church. We talked a great deal about the number of decisions in our church, and the numbers were impressive.

But we were becoming progressively less effective at assimilating new members. Our approach was imbalanced, weighted heavily toward the "bringing" but light on making disciples.

Remember: crisis inspires creativity. We used this realization of weakness as a time to reexamine our self-perception. Our conclusion? Our very *success* was creating a structure that was

> # THE MEGACHURCH IS A PASTOR KILLER. IT IS ALSO A GROWTH-INHIBITING EXPERIENCE FOR THE AVERAGE BELIEVER.

inadequate at enhancing the discipling side of church life. We needed a new definition of success.

We decided that our major problem was our basic self-definition: that of a megachurch. In my own mind, a megachurch is usually a group of 2,000 to 3,000 who are gathered around multiple programs. Usually this large membership is accompanied by a charismatic leader and very dynamic public services. In our case, this self-perception was supported by others: We were described in local newspapers as a megachurch.

We were experiencing some internal tensions that called for a change in our model for success:

- With our rapid growth, our leadership was wearing out. Our workers were overworked because our ministry focused on professional care, rather than lay care. Yet,
- Because of limited resources we could not hire more staff.
- The few lay workers we had were complaining about unclear instructions because of unavailable leaders.
- People were concerned about the mounting costs of facilities. They were asking how we could continue to develop facilities for growth without exhausting our finances.
- People were complaining about not being able to participate in major decisions.
- People expressed the lack of a sense of belonging.
- We had a need for methodical Bible studies consistently presented and shared.

All this led to my forming some definite opinions about the megachurch. It is a pastor killer. It is also a growth-inhibiting experience for the average believer. Not surprisingly, it isn't just churches of 2,000 to 3,000 that are operating on the megachurch model. Many churches of 300 to 400 emulate the model as well.

We knew we needed to move away from this model of breadth and to replace it with a model of depth. We needed to work out a definition of success that wasn't based on the number of decisions but instead allowed us to view assimilation and discipleship as measures of success while maintaining our outreach.

The Metachurch Model

We sought a consultant to help us make this shift, and we

found just the help we needed in Dr. Carl George of Fuller Church Growth Ministries. Dr. George formulated the "metachurch" model we met in an earlier chapter. This model bases ministry on members helping members, standing *with* (Greek, *meta*) each other instead of depending so much on professional help. It utilizes small groups as the means of delivering this style of ministry, rather than depending so heavily on large gatherings of the entire body.[2]

I will never forget Dr. George sharing with the core of our leadership various metaphors descriptive of a church. He said a start-up pioneer church having 40 people may be described as a mouse, while a megachurch is an elephant. Our leaders were impressed. We were an elephant-size church!

Then Carl broke the bad news. An elephant was an inadequate model for an effective church. He outlined the problems inherent in the elephant vision:

- Inability to effectively assimilate people as quickly as we reached them;
- Inability to move and respond quickly to personal problems in people's lives;
- Inability to adequately present the vision and mission of the church;
- Inability to nurture and care properly for new believers;
- Inability to train and process leaders at the pace our growth required, and to utilize them at a pace they could handle;
- A rising sense of loneliness;
- A feeling of being disenfranchised from the church's decision-making process.

Everyone was silent. Suddenly we didn't want to be an elephant church anymore. We knew we were at a crisis—one that required a new way of viewing ourselves. Although we wanted to stay at our present level of outreach, we wanted the advantages of a small church at the same time.

A Mouse-Size Model

Let me emphasize here the importance of word pictures and metaphors in communicating the need for adequate models. Dr. George had met this need with his metaphor of the elephant. He knew we needed not just information but "folklore"—stories in which we could see ourselves, complete with anecdotes that describe our situation.

Our consultant continued to describe our situation in such pictorial terms. He got a lot of laughs when he said that although we might not want to remain an elephant, neither did we want to become a dinosaur. Then he suggested a metaphor that rang true. He described a picture of a church that was more like a bunch of field mice.

Think of it. Here are hundreds of mice all huddled in small groups. They are all related, and all committed to a common purpose. The picture spoke to us of how we could remain large in numbers while staying "small" in the sense of meeting individual needs. Before long, we began to make this shift satisfactorily while still staying true to our original aim. And the ability to visualize the picture of a field of mice has been instrumental in the process.

This shift toward discipleship and assimilation through lay leadership was an adjustment for many people. Some liked the "easy believism"—the lack of demands—of the megachurch model. Others missed the professionalism of paid staff members. The shift was not without some cost, but it enabled us to respond more adequately to the Lord's command not only to evangelize but also to "make disciples of all nations,...teaching them" (Matt. 28:19,20).

Paradigms and Specific Changes

Despite the discomfort felt by some, and despite the ambiguity of wanting to remain a large church while thinking "mouse-size thoughts," Eastside's new paradigms began to take root. Following are some specific changes that facilitated the changes.

Developing a Preaching Team

We moved from having a single person of high visibility in the pulpit, to a team of presenters. This shift to a preaching *team* caused the church to focus on our mission rather than on any one leader.

This change also addressed the problem of wearing out the preacher. By distributing the task of preaching among three people, I was able to reduce the amount of stress on my life personally. This has allowed me to put more thought into the preparation and training of leaders.

Admittedly, this change also came with a price tag. Some of our members experienced symptoms of grief, but most adjusted to the new self-definition that required this change.

Small-Group Focus

Shortly after changing our self-definition we had developed 140 small groups, nearly tripling the number we had under the megachurch model. They were not an overnight hit with many. One thing that helped, however, was the leaders' willingness to implement the groups over a period of time. I will never forget the meeting where I shared this shift in focus. I said we anticipated that it would take us three to four years to get a significant percentage of the church in small groups. Everyone was greatly relieved. They could focus on where we were headed. They knew the new rules to the game. They realized it wasn't fourth quarter with 30 seconds to go.

The groups enable us to respond more quickly to the many personal needs among our members. Of course, they required that we spend a huge amount of time preparing lay leadership for them. This, too, was built into the process.

Side-Door Evangelism

Many church leaders believe that growth comes by strangers walking through the front door. Yet, every pastor who has analyzed his congregation knows that the person who walks through the front door without any prior relationship with the church is the most difficult to assimilate. At Eastside, we discovered that 90 percent of the people who allow themselves to be discipled, and who stay in our church, were brought by a friend or relative—as it were, through the side door.

Side-door evangelism is when people are brought into the church by a friend. They become involved in church on this low-key, personal level, rather than through the whole-church assemblies. This shift in our definition of evangelism has allowed us to encourage our congregation not only to bring their friends, but also to include them in their lives. This also enables members to include themselves in the more personal dynamics of church life.

I think the results of this shift will be gratifying for many decades. By focusing on inclusion, we are growing more healthily. Our program outreach leaders initially viewed this as a threat but eventually bought into the approach.

Lay-Led Programs

What a group *celebrates* defines what it considers to be a success. So at Eastside we started celebrating lay-driven ministries regularly. In a very few years we had increased our workforce to more than 1,500 people doing 2,100 different ministries. This shift was resisted by some of our members—especially those who felt they paid tithes to have professional care.

Of course, we did not eliminate professional staff but we began to use them more to train lay leaders. We refused to define ministry in an institutional way alone. We emphasized that at least 20 percent of the members in any church are gifted by Christ to be part of a group who can provide most of the care that church needs. By celebrating the layperson, ownership of this ministry has risen.

Regionalizing the Church
As part of our new direction, we organized our church into four distinct regions. We have pastors heading each region who can respond quickly through the organization of the leadership team. Our home groups are also organized by regions.

The Facilities Problem
At least two factors will continue to pose problems regarding church facilities in the future. One is the problem of rising costs. The other is the learning lag of baby boomers who are typically slow to respond to the discipline of liberal giving. Our shift in direction at Eastside included planning for ways to grow while using our present facilities for multiple uses instead of incurring debts for facilities that may decrease the quality of our ministries.

WHAT WE LEARNED: A SUMMARY

During the last five years, Eastside has expanded its definition of what we mean by church. A church of 5,000 requires an approach that is different from the church of 10 that started out in my living room. When we were a small pioneer church we were speaking of reaching many. Now when we discuss our future we emphasize mouse-size needs. To some, this feels like a change in mission. But our values have never changed.

Like ours, your church may be very effective at one or another aspect of mission, but deficient in another. To become better rounded and more effective requires that we seize new opportunities. And the first step is to identify needed shifts in the church's definition of success.

But people aren't interested in ideas alone. They are interested in personal impact. Descriptions of new and exciting paradigms must be accompanied by practical steps. We learned that these steps can lead to conflict and dissatisfaction. But because this in turn can lead to new discoveries, we learned to embrace them as a friend.

We learned that solutions to new problems cannot move ahead of:

- The lenses through which a group views reality;
- The group's definition of success;
- The group's perception of the rules of the game.

Although your specific church problems may be vastly different, I believe that solutions to them must face change in these three areas.

WHY PARADIGM SHIFTS ARE DIFFICULT

Why is it so hard for people to see the need for constructive change? Joel Barker shares a story that offers a helpful explanation. It also illustrates why the newest person in your church is likely able to be the first to see the point—why new eyes see new things.

The Chess Masters[3]
Barker tells of some research done by Herbert Simon and William C. Chase. For their experiment, they enlisted nine

chess players. Three were ranked internationally, three were intermediate players and three were novices.

The experimenters set up a partially played chess game behind a movable partition. Then the partition was removed and each subject was given five seconds to look at the board. The partition was then replaced and the subject was asked to re-create what he had seen on a blank chess board.

As you might guess, the masters did best. They averaged 81 percent accuracy in re-creating the position of the 20 chess pieces they had seen—for only five seconds. The novice chess players' performances were the poorest, having only about 33 percent accuracy.

As Barker observes, we might easily theorize from the results of this experiment that (1) master players have amazing memories; (2) playing the game well makes you better at remembering piece location; or (3) the masters have special tricks for recalling pieces.

But the experiment went on. Next, Chase and Simon arranged the chess pieces randomly by computer, no attention being paid to rules of the game. Again, the three classes of players were given the same amount of time to look at the setup and to re-create on an empty chess board what they had seen.

This time, the performances were dramatically different. The accuracy of the championship chess players plummeted. In fact, *it was worse than that of the beginners!*

Barker points out that what happened in this remarkable experiment has to do with paradigms. As long as the chess pieces were arranged "according to the rules," the master players could draw inferences of location-relationship that gave them incredible accuracy. But once the rules were ignored, the long hours the masters had spent practicing and playing were rendered useless. The chess paradigm gave them wonderful vision within the boundaries of the game. But when the paradigm was removed, the masters were masters no longer.

So it is in churches. The more effective we are, the more entrenched we become in predefined rules, and the more blind we are to our growing ineffectiveness.

....

PARADIGM PIONEERS ARE ALWAYS INQUISITIVE, HUMBLE STUDENTS. IF THEY ASSUME THE STATUS OF EXPERT, THEY CAN BE THE CHURCH'S GREATEST OBSTACLE TO GROWTH.

....

Relating this to our specific experience at Eastside, we were extremely effective in outreach to baby boomers. This was the core definition of our church. This very success, however, made us slow to realize our need to reach others. It took newer members to see a broader reality. They wanted to be assimilated. We needed a broader definition to accomplish the task. We had to stop being experts and become nondefensive learners all over again.

Paradigm pioneers are always inquisitive, humble students. If they assume the status of expert, they can be the church's greatest obstacle to growth.

BIBLICAL CHANGE AGENTS

The Bible is full of paradigm shifts led by paradigm heroes. They are characterized by being open to the leading of God's Spirit instead of being chained to past experience.

Jeremiah's Paradigm Leap

The prophet Jeremiah wasn't a very popular fellow in his time. Why? Because he described to his fellow Judeans a new paradigm—Judah under Babylonian dominion.

The armies of the Babylonian king Nebuchadnezzar were standing outside Jerusalem. The nation was clearly defeated. Under God's direction, Jeremiah took a paradigm leap. He heard the Lord say that it was time for a new lens. Not only would the Jews prosper in Babylon, but with God's people among them, the Babylonians would prosper as well.

This was a radical and novel shift toward a missions view of what Jewishness stood for. Jewishness was meant to be a blessing in all the earth. It also meant that you could be a Jew even if Jerusalem were destroyed and its inhabitants carted off to Babylonia. If you were a Jew from the heart, you could even be a Jew in Babylon. Jews had never been described in this way before. "He's demoralizing the troops," cried Jeremiah's detractors. So they tossed him in a well for seeing reality in a new way.

Jonah's Paradigm Shock

Look at the prophet Jonah. What was his problem? He couldn't see God loving the wicked citizens of Nineveh. God was supposed to love the Jews. But he was confronted with a new paradigm. The story is told with humorous irony. Nature obeyed God in the form of the storm and a great fish, pagan Ninevites obeyed God in a great moral reform, pagan sailors obeyed God, even a gourd obeyed God—but Jonah, God's prophet, did not obey Him.

In this new paradigm, God wanted to show Jonah and His people that as Jews they were to have a view of God's all-inclusive love. He was a God for all nations. Jonah must have experienced maximum paradigm shock in the belly of the great fish.

THE HINDRANCE OF HINDSIGHT

Familiarity with the past hinders our being able to visualize new paradigms. A little more than 10 years ago, a member of our congregation came to me and said, "Doug, you need a fax machine in your offices at the church."

I said, "A *what* machine?"

He said, "A fax machine. It's the new wave of the future. You can transmit copied material through the telephone line."

I thought to myself, *Now why would anyone need that?* I chuckled when he said, "We are going to make a fortune selling these services to greater Seattle."

Of course, my friend got the last laugh. Now I have a fax machine in my office at home and another at church. The offices of our senior staff are connected by fax machines. I fax information all over the world. I couldn't get by without the fax machine. It has sped up and improved my ability to send letters and articles, and allowed me to communicate immediately with friends all over the world.

My friend had the foresight to invest his money in this new opportunity. He was a paradigm pioneer. He saw a new opportunity and he seized it. I could not see the future because my vision was limited to the past.

Some time later, I learned that I wasn't the only one with this inhibition. In his book *They All Laughed*, Ira Flatow writes humorously of inventors' discoveries.[4] He relates that the fax machine was actually invented 150 years ago by Giovanni Caselli, a priest no less. Unbelievably, he established a fax line between Paris and Lyon that lasted for five years between 1865 and 1870. He was considered a nut in his time. What would a priest be doing with all of this newfangled equipment lying about the house? Caselli saw so far ahead, it took centuries to catch up.

What are the spiritual fax machines in the church's future? Will we laugh when we hear about them?

Often, what needs to be done in the church has been done before. New paradigms are often no more than a restatement of old ones, or the new application of methods long left unimplemented. Will we scoff when a young David tells us that slingshots will work better than armor? After my fax machine lesson, I determined to be more open to the future, and not to be so impressed with the limitations of the twentieth century.

Man was created by God to be creative and innovative. I was surprised to notice recently that the first descriptions of what worship services were like in the Early Church appear *two centuries* after New Testament times. In the New Testament itself, every sermon is aimed at seekers and attuned to their varying needs. I wonder if it isn't by strategic design that we don't know what the earliest believers did in church.

God awaits our innovation and creativity at adapting our services to the changing needs of our audiences. If it is not forbidden in Scripture, it is allowed. Having outreach for Him in mind, we have no need to fear innovation as a church. The future is ours.

THE PARABLE OF THE TWINS[5]

Once upon a time, twin boys were conceived in their mother's womb. Weeks passed and the twins developed. As their awareness grew, they laughed for joy: "Isn't it great that we were conceived? Isn't it great to be alive?"

Together the twins explored their world. When they found that the umbilical cord passed life along to them from their mother, they sang for joy: "How great is our mother's love, that she shares her own life for us."

As weeks stretched into months, the twins noticed how much each was changing. "What does it mean?" asked one twin.

"It means that our stay in this world is drawing to an end," said the other.

"But I don't want to go. I want to stay here always."

"We have no choice," said the other. "And maybe there is life after birth!"

"But how can there be? We will shed our life-cord, and how is life possible without it? Besides, no one has ever returned to the womb to tell us that there is life after birth. No, this is the end."

And so the one twin fell into despair: "If conception ends in birth, what is the purpose of life in the womb? It is meaningless! Maybe there is no mother at all."

"But there *has* to be," protested the other. "How else did we get here? How do we remain alive?"

"Have you ever actually seen our mother?" said the one. "Maybe she lives only in our minds. Maybe we made her up, because the idea made us feel good."

And so the last days in the womb were filled with deep questioning and fear. Finally, the moment of birth arrived. And when the twins had passed from their world, they opened their eyes. They cried with joy, for what they saw exceeded their fondest dreams.

"No eye has seen, no ear has heard, no mind has conceived what God has prepared for those who love him" (1 Cor. 2:9).

PARADIGMS *in* PRACTICE

1. Focus on the specific kind of innovation you would like to see in your church. Let your imagination free as you visualize the change "folklore" style—by means of a morality tale, a parable, an animal story.

2. In what areas have you discovered that being an "expert" can blind people to new truths?

3. How would you define your church 10 years from now? How would you articulate this new vision in two sentences?

Notes

1. "The Innovator That Quit Innovating," *U. S. News and World Report,* Aug. 31, 1992, pp. 23ff.
2. For further information about the metachurch, see Carl George, *Prepare Your Church for the Future* (Grand Rapids, MI: Fleming H. Revell Co., 1991).
3. Joel Barker, *Future Edge: Discovering New Paradigms of Success* (New York: William Morrow and Company, 1992), pp. 103-105.
4. Ira Flatow, *They All Laughed* (New York: HarperCollins, 1993).
5. "Parable of the Twins," author unknown.

7

....

BIBLICAL PARADIGM SHIFTS

In this chapter, we want to add to the several instances we have already noted when paradigm shifts were called for in Scripture. Yet, we should not suppose that the Bible is our only source for these models. They also abound in the "secular" world, and if we are careful to ask whether these paradigm shifts are not contrary to the teachings of Scripture, we are free to learn from them as well.

As we have noted, William Carey modeled the modern missionary movement after the Hudson Bay Company's use of agents. Paul's Epistles are loaded with terms and concepts taken directly from his experience in the marketplace. Because all truth is God's truth (see Jas. 1:17), if an insight from outside Scripture does not violate a scriptural principle, it can be pressed into the service of the Church (see 1 Cor. 9:22).

But we should especially be interested in understanding biblical examples of paradigm shifts. Throughout the Bible, God's people are often portrayed as the most current and innovative of all people.

The evangelical faith itself is a call to a radical paradigm shift. John 3:3 is a radical statement of the shift necessary to enter the kingdom of God. Jesus said, "No one can see the kingdom of God unless he is born again." Pretty radical stuff! Jesus is saying that the shift of perspective required to enter His kingdom is so intense that it can be described as a rebirth.

Faith is the stuff of perpetual transformation. If our trust in God is limited to the ways of the past, how can we remain faithful in the future? Being born again is not just a moment of crisis, it is a lifestyle. Vision-oriented, change-friendly church leaders of today can be encouraged that leaders in the Bible faced similar challenges.

THE SHIFT IN THE CHURCH'S ETHNICITY

Let's look more closely at the shocking paradigm shift the apostle Peter confronted in Acts 10. Peter was summoned to the home of Cornelius, a Gentile officer in the Roman army. Earlier, God had given Peter a vision, calling on him to eat of clean and unclean animals without discrimination. Meanwhile, Cornelius and his family had been prepared by the Holy Spirit to become Christians. They had presented so many alms, they had reached all the way to heaven as a memorial to their devotion to God. Cornelius got God's attention. Now, God was about to get Peter's attention.

"Who Can Stop This?"

Obeying God's command to go to Cornelius's house, Peter began to share the gospel with these Gentiles. As he did so, the Holy Spirit fell on them—and Gentiles received the gift of tongues that the Jewish followers of Christ had received at Pentecost (10:44-46)! The vision of eating reptiles was nothing compared to the reality facing Peter—Gentiles joining Christ's Church!

I wonder if Peter's question wasn't asked partly in dismay: "Can anyone keep these people from being baptized with water? They have received the Holy Spirit just as we have" (Acts 10:47). So he ordered that Cornelius and his household be baptized in the name of Jesus Christ. And when they asked Peter to stay on for a few days and teach them, he did.

Here is one of the most profound paradigm shifts ever witnessed. Christianity had just entered a new stage. It was no

PAUL'S ESTABLISHING PREDOMINANTLY GENTILE CHURCHES PRECIPITATED THE FIRST EARLY CHURCH CONVENTION, AS RECORDED IN ACTS 15.

longer a subsect of Judaism. The Church was no longer the singular domain of the Jew. Neither would it be allowed to separate, having one Church for Jews and another for Gentiles.

As always, some were frightened by all this change. Peter was called back to headquarters in Acts 11. He wondered how he would explain this series of events. In a stunning defense to his peers, he explained that it was the Holy Spirit who had forced the shift upon them. "Who was I to think that I could oppose God?" he asked (v. 17).

Meanwhile, God was already preparing another radical shift. Just as He would not allow the Church to be only a Jewish sect, neither would He settle for its being limited to Palestine. It must be a worldwide expression.

Because of the experience with Cornelius, Peter grasped the concept of a Jew-Gentile church to some extent, but it is clear that he was not going to be the enthusiastic paradigm pioneer the Church needed. The stage was set, but there was no leader. They had seen an event. They had observed an experience. But they had no model to use in understanding the overall significance of Gentiles being included in God's new covenant.

Whom could God use to direct this monumental paradigm shift?

Paul, the Paradigm Pioneer

As we know from our vantage point, the true paradigm pioneer was Paul. He and his team were commissioned by the Jerusalem church in Acts 13:1,2, and the next two chapters detail their glorious experiences on the first missionary tour.

Paul's establishing these predominantly Gentile churches precipitated the first Early Church convention, as recorded in Acts 15. The apostolic leaders in Jerusalem had no doubt that God was at work. But how should they interpret His fruitfulness with non-Jews? No doubt their hearts and minds were stretched, trying to interpret what God was doing. Something new was afoot. New ways of explaining the gospel were required. Models were needed to ensure the Church's integrity.

As the first Jew/Gentile church, the church in Antioch provided a secondary stage for the shift to a predominantly Gentile Church worldwide (see Acts 11:19-26). Paul and Barnabas were part of this church and part of the leadership that pointed the way to new models of church growth.

Peter's Reluctance

Where was Peter in this process? He was the one who had experienced the first call to make this paradigm shift. But apparently he was unable to fully accept it. Later, in the book of Galatians, we learn that when he was around Jews he would be a Jew, and when he was with Gentiles he would be a Gentile. Paul rebuked him strongly (see Gal. 2:11ff.).

Peter's real problem was that he was unable to commit himself completely to the new paradigm. The Church needed an entirely new set of explanations for what was happening. But by hanging on to the old while affirming the new, Peter was blurring the radical difference between the two paradigms. It took decades for the Church to work this out.

One Wednesday night, we were finishing up two alarming passages in the Gospel of Luke—the temptation of Jesus in chapter 3, and the exorcism of the man in chapter 4 (see vv. 31-37). One of our new followers of Christ asked, "Do you think the devil attacks us new Christians more than older Christians?"

I paused to consider a response and was so caught off guard by my own answer that I thought about it the whole drive home. Scratching my nose nervously I answered, "No, I don't think so. But the attacks are different. When you are a new believer, Satan tries to take advantage of you based on what you don't know. More mature Christians, on the other hand, are attacked based on what we do know. So none of us can allow ourselves to be smug."

Satan attacked Peter at the point of what he "knew"—a paradigm in which God worked among the Jews. He was comfortable in that framework. What he knew got in his way. It appears he was never able to hurdle the obstacles of his own mind. The movement still needed a leader.

The apostle Paul appeared as the new leader because he saw the crisis of Acts 10 as an opportunity. In addition to his renewed eyesight, he received a new heart—which is often required in order to see new truth. Paul's heart was softened by grace, and his mind became capable of anticipating the unpredictable.

Summing Up
What changed for the Church in this new paradigm? Almost

everything. Its view of the Law was changed—reduced to a few simple commands. Gentiles were not to eat blood offered to idols, nor to indulge in sexual immorality (see Acts 15:19,20,29). No longer was circumcision required. This represented a significant simplification for the sake of a new paradigm. A people committed to God without circumcision was inconceivable to many of the early Jewish church leaders. But their new situation required it.

The radical and controversial nature of these changes are often glossed over in our Bible studies, and the principle they represent lies unapplied to our present situation. The incident is actually a paradigm shift of volcanic proportions, one that illustrates that the Early Church was eventually able to be flexible enough to keep it vibrant for centuries.

Let's specify some of the changes through which Paul guided the church with his great vision.

- He supplied the Church with new lenses through which to view Jews and Gentiles.
- The ancient requirement of circumcision was dropped.
- The boundaries and definitions of success were extended beyond Judea into the whole world.

Let's diagram the Early Church's experiences:

What flexibility in the Church all this called for! What a work of the Holy Spirit was required to enact such changes! The changes God wanted to make were very threatening to some of the Church's leaders. Just as in our own congregations, some must have felt stripped of their presuppositions and left exposed and naked in the open space between old and new paradigms. Yet, the Spirit eventually implemented a tremendous paradigm shift. The same Spirit wants to invade our own hearts and to lead us to similar heights of creativity. Can we expect any less of ourselves than was required of these early leaders?

A LIBERATION PARADIGM

The book of Exodus demonstrates another powerful biblical paradigm—a paradigm of liberation. It is the bedrock of the history of salvation.

For centuries, the people of God had been captive in Egypt as slaves. Suddenly, within a matter of days, they were released as a free nation. The experience created a paradigm shock from which some did not recover. Many Israelites had difficulty accepting Moses' message, "Free at last!" Even in their agony, they had been slaves for so long that freedom had no meaning.

Poor Moses! He was having a terrible time discovering what it meant to be a leader. He had tried to be a deliverer once on

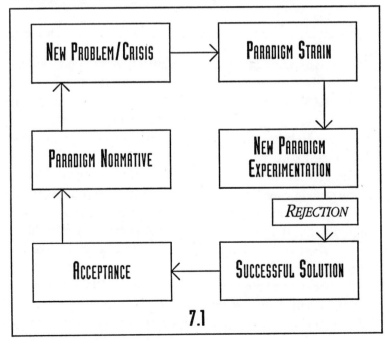

7.1

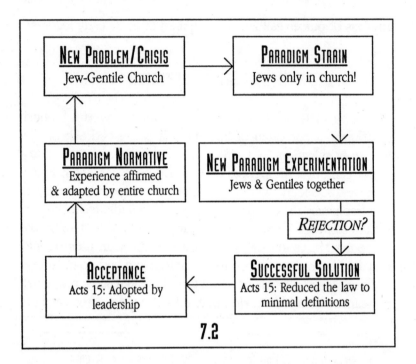

7.2

his own when he had tried to break up the fight between two of his brethren. Now, fresh from the wilderness of Midian, seeing himself again as a tool in God's hand was frightening. To make matters worse, Pharaoh had the maniacal idea of punishing the Hebrews by requiring them to make bricks without straw (see Exod. 5:7).

The account is filled with miracles, crowned by the parting of the waters (see Exod. 14). As Israel burst through the Red Sea on dry ground, they turned to see the Egyptian armies engulfed by the waters. Surely the event would radically change their view of reality. God was at work on their behalf. God could part the seas!

The incident reminds me of the first time I talked to a person who had been dramatically healed. A case of lupus had been healed by prayer in a Kathryn Kuhlman crusade. Doctors had confirmed the healing. There was no denying it. It changed my whole view of how God works. This opened a whole new world for me. God could heal (see Jas. 5:14-16). He could do anything, and I could be part of what He was doing!

But in the case of the Israelites, it was only a matter of days before the Israelites were crying out for the onions and leeks and fleshpots of Egypt (see Num. 11:5). Why? They had no structure or model within their self-definition to understand themselves as free people. They were good at being slaves. But this freedom stuff was tough. Now they were called to see themselves in a new way—a requirement that an entire generation failed to meet. Only after their generation died in the wilderness did the people develop a paradigm set that would allow them to live consistently with what God had done.

It often works the same way in the Church. The greatest miracle may be to persuade a group of slaves to venture beyond their comfort zone.

What are the Red Seas you or your congregation face? Our own Red Sea crossing may be the rescue of a marriage, the salvation of a child, experiencing financial victory or the deliverance of a church in captivity to past ways of thinking. Whatever our crossing, God wants to use such experiences to broaden and deepen our understanding of His power. But internalizing such experiences requires growth, and growth requires change.

ARE WE GRASSHOPPERS OR GIANTS?

Two marvelous men—Joshua and Caleb—became paradigm pioneers when Israel approached the Promised Land. Let's allow their story, from Numbers 13:26-53, to challenge us.

Recall that God had led the Israelites through the wilderness to the border of Canaan. He told Moses to send some men to spy on the land God had promised to give them.

Joshua and Caleb were two of those spies. They explored the dry and barren Negev in the south and the hill country in central Palestine. They spied on the towns and the cities, the agricultural prospects and the people. Then:

> They came back to Moses and Aaron and the whole Israelite community at Kadesh in the Desert of Paran. There they reported to them and to the whole assembly and showed them the fruit of the

ALL PARADIGM PIONEERS HAVE A DIFFERENT SPIRIT FROM THE NAYSAYERS ABOUT THEM. THEY HAVE THE ABILITY TO SEE A NEW THING, TO PERCEIVE A BRIGHT FUTURE, TO TAP INTO THE POWER OF GOD.

> land. They gave Moses this account: "We went into the land to which you sent us, and it does flow with milk and honey! Here is its fruit. But the people who live there are powerful, and the cities are fortified and very large. We even saw descendants of Anak there" (Num. 13:26-28).

The good report caused quite a stir among the people. Caleb silenced them and said, "We should go up and take possession of the land, for we can certainly do it" (v. 30). But other spies from the expedition protested, saying, "We can't attack those people; they are stronger than we are" (v. 31). Their report was more negative. "Yes, it's a good land, but populated with giants so huge we looked like grasshoppers!" (see vv. 32,32).

What a small view of themselves—grasshoppers! Only Joshua and Caleb in the entire nation of Israel were able to make the paradigm shift to non-grasshopperdom. They made the hard journey from being slaves to promise holders. They had "a different spirit" (14:24). All paradigm pioneers have a different spirit from the naysayers about them. They have the ability to see a new thing, to perceive a bright future, to tap into the power of God.

The fact that an entire generation of doubting, fearful Israelites were left languishing in the wilderness is a clear warning of the dangers of refusing to shift to a new reality. Could we be facing the same threat? The answer is an emphatic *yes!* In every era, we are placed in situations that are similar to the experience of the Jews in Numbers 14. We are asked to view ourselves as a people indwelt by the Holy Spirit, not as grasshoppers.

TESTING THE SPIRIT OF CHANGE

"So, Murren," you say. "Are you saying we ought to buy into every new idea that comes along?" No, absolutely not! Any shift in the Church must be based on biblical values. We do not make changes just because something "works"—we can never buy into the gospel of utilitarianism. The driving force of all Spirit-led paradigm shifts are the values of Christ's kingdom. His purpose for us is made very clear. We are to:

- Glorify God (see Eph. 1:17);
- Show that people matter to Him (see Matt. 25:31-46);
- Love Him and others from the heart (see Matt. 19:19);
- Heal, accept and restore fallen humanity to God (see John 8:3-11);

- Reconcile men to God, and men to men (see 2 Cor. 5:18);
- Radically submit to the will of the King of the kingdom (see Matt. 7:21).

Change must be driven by these kinds of values. By the same token, if these values aren't apparent among us, we need to pray for eyes to see how we can change in order to incorporate them. And let's face it: There are times when our systems no longer glorify God. There are times when our systems don't show people that they matter to God. And there are plenty of occasions where we are no longer communicating intelligibly God's love to humans. At these times, we need to look around for new paradigms.

What we do or how we do it and when we do it are negotiable. The reasons we do what we do are not.

What crises and problems does the Church face today? What new church strategies must we face, such as the apostle Paul did? What new ground can we navigate if we have the courage to face the challenges of the giants in the land? Just knowing shifts have occurred in the Bible is a great comfort to me. In these accounts, we see a change-friendly pattern. Good news! Others have gone ahead of us!

PARADIGMS *in* PRACTICE

1. When and how does your church have baptisms? Was the choice of this practice based on a specific problem? How can the baptismal services be improved? Would changing anything about them hurt anything? Can you anticipate how people would react to changing them?

2. If your church did not have a building, how would it grow?

3. Would you characterize your church as exhibiting the spirit of Joshua and Caleb or that of the 10 spies? If many members have a "grasshopper mentality," what can be done about it?

4. Are you facing any changes that are as dramatic as the situations faced in Acts 10—13? If so, can you identify them and articulate them clearly to the newest person in your church?

CRISIS/NEW PROBLEM
The Diaspora

↓

NEW SOLUTIONS
Jewishness defined as matter of the heart

↓

NEW PARADIGMS
The remnant rejects the new paradigm in Jerusalem

↓

NEW PARADIGMS EMERGE
A Jew can be a Jew in Babylon

↓

ADAPTATION
Definition of a Jew
Book of Daniel is canonized as a
pattern of Jewishness for many generations

7.3

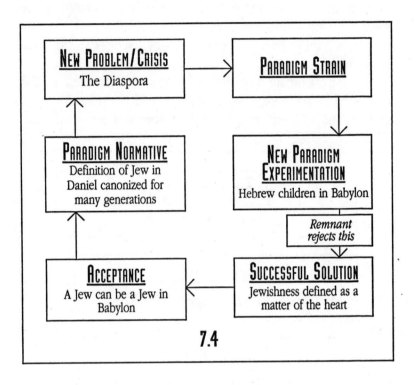

7.4

8

....

ANTICIPATING SHIFTS

The failure to anticipate the need for paradigm shifts exacts a high price from the Church. At Eastside, we have missed vital opportunities to reach our community because new needs caught us napping, and we were unable to retool quickly enough to meet them. It is an agonizing feeling—something like riding a bus and suddenly realizing you've driven by all the stops. Anticipating the future allows for better preparation

Anticipation isn't just an intuitive skill. It is one that can be practiced and learned. Peter Schwartz suggests that in order to learn to anticipate the future, it's necessary to "live backwards." He says, "Leading from the long view is the call of the leader."[1] Living today with your future in mind can change a lot of priorities.

Maybe, on a personal level, this is what David had in mind when he said, "Teach us to number our days" (Ps. 90:12). What will you be like at age 85? What phases or cycles do you think you might go through between now and then? What do you believe is most important for you in the meantime?

Churches should ask similar questions. Churches also have limited lifetimes, and they may go through several phases—even a few births and rebirths. Churches with a vision for their future are usually more effective today.

AN EXERCISE IN LIVING BACKWARD

Our church leadership decided to see if we could visualize what we would look like 30 years in the future. We tried to project ourselves to the year 2020. It wasn't easy. The process was like peeling an onion—backward.

At first, we were all so focused on current issues that it took us hours to escape them. But eventually we did, and it turned out to be one of the most valuable exercises we've ever done as a team.

Our visionizing ran the spectrum of our experience. We asked questions such as, What will our facilities look like in 2020? What present trends will likely continue? And, How might these trends affect our church life? How would the money issue affect our church in the future? What if the Gross National Product of the United States stayed at 1.4 percent, as it did in the spring of 1992, for a decade? Will there be any opportunities in demographical changes that we could anticipate in five-year increments?

By asking such questions, and by living our church life from the end backward, we saw many things that we hadn't seen before.

Our Church in the Future

There we were, church leaders in a nonsmoke-filled room, having white board and felt pen ready, a few imaginative minds prepared to venture out into the year 2020.

Doug (Yes, this is me): "Let's go forward to the year 2010 and chart out our present growth rate. Let's assume that we can't achieve the rate we've enjoyed the last few years, so let's reduce it by a half or a third in the future."

Mike: "Let's choose one-third. It sounds better to me."

Lucky: "Sounds good to me."

(As you can tell, the enthusiasm wasn't building yet. One must be patient in these processes. The visionary types tend to threaten the more stable members of the group, and the stable ones tend to frustrate the visionaries.)

By visualizing ourselves in the year 2010 and charting our past, we found that we would total (at our present rate of growth) 20,000 members. By 2020, we could number between 30,000 and 40,000.

We all thought, *Are you kidding?*

The first question arose.

Doug: "O.K., here's another question. How will these sheer numbers affect our church life? What critical junctures will we have faced? What could make us want to continue at this rate?"

Lucky: "Let's add some questions: How will our community view a church of this size? Could a church of that size present obstacles in perception that would diffuse our message? What focus might we need to be prepared to consider in order to avoid pitfalls and still reach the lost?"

We all nodded, agreeing that these were good questions.

Mike: "Well, it's likely that a church of 20,000 people won't be all that uncommon in the years 2010 to 2020 if current trends continue. It is very likely we will have many, many churches of 40 to 100, few churches of 100 to 800, and many churches in excess of 5,000 to 10,000 people."

Lucky: "Yes, but isn't the trend now for larger churches to find a way to remain 'smaller'? It isn't just the size that will make the difference, but how the size is presented."

Doug: "I think you're right. You know, 15 years ago a church of 2,000 was considered immense. What if, in 2020, a church of 20,000 is considered no more unusual than a church of 2,000 or 3,000 is today? The identity crisis would be eased."

Mike: "I don't think so. I think there are some unique dilemmas that you face in a church that size, just in terms of identity."

We began to list some of these problems. After 20 or 30 minutes, we tired of this question and went to the next one. It is good not to get bored in this process.

Ministry in the Future

Doug: "O.K., let's take another question. How would we have to change our paradigm of a church staff in a church of 8,000, versus how we view staff in a church today of, say, 4,000?"

Lucky: "I think that we would want to look at being able to divide up the members into smaller units. So my guess is that from the 8,000 mark on, the kind of staff person we'll be looking for radically changes. It seems to me that we'd be looking for a facilitator/trainer instead of a superstar performer."

Doug: "Eureka! I've got it. We need to have a church that is regionalized—let's say in four sections. Sort of like districts in a political caucus of sorts. We could easily divide ourselves up into 8 to 10 sections later. Maybe over the next five years we could even begin developing this presentation of church life that could prepare us for this time."

Mike: "That sounds exciting."

Lucky: "It sounds like a regional application of anticipating what problems we face in the future. Regionalizing would increase the effectiveness of our small groups and also allow for quicker response to developing disciples. The central site remains the gathering place for the unchurched, for the inspiration of believers, but the real action begins to work in these regions."

Doug: "I think this is an adaptation of something Carl

George has spoken to us about, isn't it?"

Lucky: "Absolutely. No one is original, you know."

Out of this planning session we came up with a list of the kinds of pastors we would need over the next four to five years. We also began to define the kinds of lay leaders this growing church would require. We saw many differences in

THE OLD ADAGE IS TRUE: "IT TAKES 14 SESSIONS TO UNLEARN WRONG CONCEPTS, THEN 7 SESSIONS TO TEACH NEW ONES."

the leaders of the future compared with those of today. We developed training models that allowed us to prepare this kind of new leader. We concluded that one mistake we had made was continually preparing leaders who were well equipped for today's problems, but ill equipped to face the impact of our future.

We continue to this day to take the "long view" in developing our church life. It is helping us to improve our ability to anticipate change.

CHURCH SIZE IN THE FUTURE

Some of you are probably saying that this exercise sounds great for a large church. The fact is that living from the end of your existence backward can help any size church. Churches of 100 to 800 are in a terrific position to capitalize on today's opportunities, so it is all the more critical for them to address these questions.

One can anticipate the kinds of fears that a congregation of 100 people will be facing in the year 2010. We know that anxiety about retirement will be high. What answers can the Church offer at that time? On average, boomers today are worth much less financially than they were in the 1980s. It doesn't look good. But we can help if we anticipate questions and develop answers.

A church of 100 will consist of people who are facing some of the greatest fears in their lives. With its membership aging, people will need comfort, belonging and mutual care. What attitudes and practices would we have to change in order to reach them?

The future may show that a church of 100 is the most effective size. Or will it be a church of 600? Or 20,000? Who knows? No doubt all sizes will be needed. The issue is *how we do church*, not how big we are.

Learning to Be Time Conscious

Church leaders must be sensitive to the time element when planning for paradigm shifts. At Eastside, we learned that it takes three to four years for our church to implement and enact any paradigm shift. We found the adage to be true: "It takes 14 sessions to unlearn wrong concepts, then 7 sessions to teach new ones."

As you saw in the previous snapshot, we concluded that dividing our church into four regions was the way we could achieve our dreams. Yet, at this writing, we are only partially through the transition. We don't really plan to be fully transitioned for another three to four years. But we are starting to explain the concept now so we will all be on the same page when the time arrives for full implementation.

Can you wait for transitions? Major paradigm shifts don't happen quickly.

How will preaching styles have changed by the year 2020? Already we can observe attitudinal shifts in our audiences every five years. The needs we must address shift constantly and may well require a change in the kind of messages that are shared.

The definition of a pastor may change radically. Our present model is taking 10 to 20 years off our lives! But would your church sustain a change?

A New Breed of Ministers?

I must share one final snapshot from our planning session. We wrapped up the meeting by discussing a broader concern regarding the kinds of ministers the church of the future will need.

Doug: "I think we need to do this about every three months to stay on track and focus our resources."

Mike: "What shall we call it?"

Doug: "Let's call it 'Living from a Long View.' Or as one author has said, 'living in the future perfect.'[2] But how many people should we share it with?"

Mike: "I don't think that many people, even in our leadership, could handle this."

Doug: "Yeah, I think you're right. I think there's so much information overload around that it requires a certain mind-set to feel comfortable with this process. Choosing the right people to be included in this process is vital."

Mike: "What if we spent the next three to four years developing 20 to 100 people who could understand this kind of thinking so we could have people who would begin to develop an ability to shift through paradigms and lead us strongly into our future? I think we have intelligent laypeople who would love to be part of this process."

Doug: "What would happen if more churches were able to anticipate what lies ahead for them? Imagine being able to focus your resources and anticipate the kind of leaders you're going to need in your future. Boy, I wish we had thought of this five years ago!"

There is a constant need to till the soil of a common vision in which to grow the seeds of unity.

Lucky: "I think we would see a whole lot less tension and far more fruitfulness if more churches did live from the end back."

Mike: "I think all this makes a new place for sociologists as church leaders."

Doug: "Absolutely—as well as historians. We need new models, new opportunities, new patterns, but we also need the experiences of our past."

Mike: "One closing question. How can we find out what our populace will look like in the year 2020?"

Doug: "There's plenty of information available. Forecasting is happening all the time. Let's go to some of the business sectors and collect some of their data. I saw a report in one of the local businesses that was trying to anticipate the labor pool that would be available in the future. This kind of data could be helpful for us in anticipating the kind of person that would likely be a candidate for our church in the coming years."

Mike: "We are really talking about a lifestyle, aren't we?

Learning to make thinking about the future should be a normal part of being a church leader."

Doug: "I think radical shifts happen so often these days that leaders must look to their own ability to see into the future. I think that one of the definitions of our core leadership in our future will be persons who are comfortable with this process of living in the long view—people who are influencers from a faith perspective. You know, Joshua and Caleb types. We need that kind of paradigm pioneer today."

THE BENEFITS OF ANTICIPATING CHANGE

Let's review the benefits of having church leaders who anticipate shifts.

Clarifying the Church's Mission

When your congregation knows where it's going, its mission is clearer to all. After all, it's a miracle for any group of people to share a common vision. It is highly unnatural for people to work together toward a common goal. There is a constant need to till the soil of a common vision in which to grow the seeds of unity.

If people know they are part of a congregation committed to the unchurched, they can focus on that call. If they view themselves as a church-planting church, they can focus on that mission. Knowing the future requirements of their mission can enable them to look forward to something exciting.

Stating a future paradigm energizes a group, while trying to be all things to all people saps energy and decreases effectiveness. Limiting boundaries enables a church to focus more specifically on resources. A group prepared to anticipate the future will experience less anxiety when future problems arrive.

Clarifying a church's future mission often enables it to remain effective through multiple pastorates. The people have a common vision that supersedes a specific leader. They will call subsequent pastors based on their commitment to the already-established mission, vision and paradigm of the church itself.

Increasing paradigm awareness in a church means that far less energy will be spent in self-definition in times of crises. For example, our church knows that we are a "bringing and including" church. We are an outreach-oriented church focused on bringing people into an environment of love, acceptance and forgiveness. Sharing this simple mission frequently in word pictures helps us a great deal. We can struggle at a number of things, but we can't slip at "bringing and including."

We are also a church committed to innovation. We are primarily focused on a single generation—baby boomers. When these definitions are clear, people are able to get on board with a common vision. Sharing our anticipation of what may lie ahead must keep in view the impact on our essential targeted audience.

Allaying Conflict and Fear

Anticipating paradigm shifts because of demographic changes is a common problem. Conflict often arises, for example, when a specific ethnic group begins to be targeted without warning.

Other shifts are more subtle. What if an industry closed in your community, causing many families to move and decreasing the population by 25 percent? This has happened in many cities in the Northwest. It is vital to anticipate the changes this kind of event can bring to a congregation. Knowing why things have changed reduces finger-pointing and conflict.

Paradigm collisions can also occur when a church is not adequately prepared for the opposite "problem"—rapid growth. When churches move from 400 to 600 members, everything changes. Usually these changes aren't evident to lay leaders for a while. My observation is that such conflicts rise to the surface within one or two years of rapid growth.

If you desire to move through these thresholds, talk to pastors who have experienced the shift. Ask them what has changed about the way they do church. Make a list of what you'll not be able to do when you are larger. You can anticipate some conflict from people who feel that being a much larger church will require them to give up some things, such as access to the senior pastor. Some may be upset when services are "streamlined," or when they cannot share songs they have personally written.

By being able to describe potential changes, fear and conflict can be allayed. Showing why these shifts will occur leads the focus away from personalities. A common problem can be grappled with by all concerned. When and if the crisis occurs, positive solutions can be waiting.

Targeting Resources Effectively
Conflict often arises about where the money will be spent. Deciding which programs will receive the largest portion of a budget can bring the worst out of a church. Passions run high at such times.

Priorities clearly adhere to paradigms. Being an outreach-oriented church is costly. We know, for example, that the typically slow way baby boomers respond to tithing means that we will need to carry every new disciple financially anywhere from six months to three years. A businessman in our congregation has anticipated that at first it will cost us anywhere from $400 to $2,400 to care for each person who makes a decision to be a follower of Christ.

As populations shift, grow and decline, and as communities change, new opportunities appear. This challenges the status quo by demanding more funds. Having clear paradigms of what your church is, and how that will be either threatened or enhanced in the future, can allow you to target resources far more effectively.

Lifting Your Church's Morale

Morale is the most intangible resource in any congregation. By morale, we mean a sense of well-being and the conviction that the future is bright. High morale manifests itself in a sense that we are winning. People don't want to lose.

Every growing congregation has high levels of this intangible resource. No congregation can exist long without it. Sometimes churches must reach way back in their history to find any. But a present sense of well-being is necessary for success.

Wise church leaders will define the target clearly for the congregation and lead them in celebration when it is hit. Morale rises measurably when progress is celebrated. Paradigms allow a church to define success in a way that all can enjoy it. It's a mood elevator for a group to have an awareness that "We've accomplished something!" Anticipation is a tool the skilled leader will use in maintaining morale.

Churches that have low morale usually have not clearly defined the boundaries of success. How does your church know it is winning at being and doing church? By anticipating paradigm shifts, success can be defined even in dynamic change. By anticipating what the new obstacles will be, new solutions can be prepared in advance.

SELECTING MODELS EFFECTIVELY

In New Testament times, local churches were established as mission outposts. They were called to adapt themselves creatively to the needs of their communities.

What does your locale require in a church? This question is vital in establishing your effectiveness. For example, Latino communities require churches that are fitted and suited to the Latino culture. Urban churches require an urban format. Blue-collar communities require quite different forms of leadership in church life than many white-collar congregations.

Anticipating changes in your community or changes within the scope and size of your own church can allow you to choose models that will work better for you. The community in which God has placed you should determine your paradigm of church more than your denomination or personal tastes.

A book that offers valuable help in selecting an effective model for the church is *Nine American Lifestyles* by Arnold Mitchell.[3] This book is based on VALS Research (Value in Lifestyles Studies, by Stanford University). Another important resource is *The Clustering of America* by Michael J. Weiss.[4]

Both of these reports show that there are many types of people in the United States. Weiss has identified 40 different neighborhood types across the country. Mitchell outlines nine approaches to life. Let's take a look at them:

Need-Driven Groups
Survivor Lifestyles
Sustainer Lifestyles

Outer-Directed Groups
Belonger Lifestyle
Emulator Lifestyle
Achiever Lifestyle

Inner-Directed Groups
I-Am-Me Lifestyle
Experimental Lifestyle
Societal Conscious Lifestyle

Combined Outer/Inner-Directed Groups
Integrated Lifestyle[5]

I include this proof of variety among people in our society

to reinforce the reasoning that not all churches can reach all people. Tools such as VALS assist us in focusing our resources boldly and effectively to match our own mission.

Our own locale at Eastside required a church that would focus on a highly seeker-sensitive ministry. Yours may require a church for the lost who are churched. There just aren't that many Christians to pass around in our communities, and the churches that make deliberate choices on lifestyles they want to attract will do a better job of reaching specific groups.

Many of our members have friends who choose not to be part of our outreach emphasis. Eventually, our congregation was prepared to accept this fact of life without giving or receiving recrimination.

We simply do not feel we can effectively reach some lifestyles and groups in our population. A strong Oriental population has begun moving into our area recently. We believe this population will require different kinds of churches. Ours isn't likely to reach them effectively. We are, however, poised to assist any other church that seeks to reach these people groups.

Neither is Eastside likely to minister to large numbers of octogenarians. We have not been all that effective in reaching retirement-age people. As I have stated, our research showed that the largest portion of unchurched people in our community were baby boomers. Yet, a significant number of these people claimed to be born again. So we knew that a significant portion of our populace were nominal Christians who were unchurched. Reaching them is our primary focus.

Different Models Are OK

Several years ago, a gentleman came from another congregation to our church. He was very frustrated by his past experience. This gave me some concern when I learned of his desire to be a leader in our congregation.

His complaint against his previous church was that it was

only a hospital. People were either born into that church or healed in it. They never grew, he said.

I asked him what the leaders felt the mission of the church was. Primarily, it was to be a hospital, he said. Then I told him that I thought that if they achieved their mission—if people were healed—then they were successful.

This took him aback. I pointed out that his paradigm of church was a place for maturing individuals. He probably viewed a church primarily as a classroom experience. I pointed out that our community, because of the proliferation of cults, had a great need for healing. Many Christians needed a place to get their spiritual legs back under them. Eastside had anticipated the situation and was matching the needs of our area.

As you probably suspected, our paradigm of the church's mission didn't satisfy this man's vision very well, either. And that's OK! Both the congregation I lead and the previous one he was in had clearly described how they would define success. He was free to move on and find a place that matched his paradigm. We remain friends today.

Churches who are aware of who they are and the needs of their community reduce a great deal of confusion and save a lot of precious energy normally given to keeping people happy.

SHIING WITH THE HILL

I started learning to ski when I was 41. Recently, I was reviewing some notes I took following my ski lessons. My only entry during the first two days was, "Sweat." We walked sideways up and down a hill for four hours straight. Then we skied on one ski as far as we could. My friend Buck Herring became my teacher on the third day. Besides clearing out most of the people in a lift-line once, I did OK.

My notes from the fourth day said, "Anticipate." I had tried to apply this one simple lesson the entire day. Anticipation allows a skier to go *with* the hill rather than fighting it. I saw one guy flying down the slope with his ski instructor behind him yelling, *"Anticipate!"*

Leading has many parallels to skiing. Being a leader requires anticipation. If you can anticipate changes, you can prepare adjustments in your paradigms. You can't look down. You've got to look ahead.

The predominant model of what church leaders are to do is largely a *responsive* model. George Barna, the noted church researcher, has said that only 4 percent of pastors in the United States view themselves as visionary leaders. You can neither ski nor lead well if you're only responsive to immediate needs and never look ahead. If the only question you are asking is, "What does the board want?" you will miss opportunities. Leaders look ahead and prepare road maps through rough terrain.

BUDGETING CHANGE

Early in our growth at Eastside, we were able to change on a dime. Our church was used to change. In fact, we used to joke about it. We would recognize a new opportunity and see how quickly we could capitalize on it.

But over the years we've discovered the importance of "budgeting" change—lessening the degree of change we make at one time. Twentieth-century people are shell-shocked by the sheer amount of change around them. They have a high level of safety needs in this information age. So we have had to be more economical about changes.

A leader's failure to anticipate the shock and pain of change will increase the already existing hyper-fear many people have toward change. Churches that have too many unanticipated changes thrust upon them become weary. A drain in spiritual energies inhibits outreach and spiritual growth. By anticipating paradigm shifts and budgeting your response to them, your church can maintain a higher level of stability. Deliberate paradigm management can allow a church to grow through many thresholds without being jarred from completing its mission.

PARADIGMS in PRACTICE

1. What kind of church is needed in your community? What people groups have you discovered that your church is most likely to reach? Are you more gifted at targeting blue-collar or white-collar populations?

2. What changes do you anticipate in your community in the next five years? Ten years? How can you prepare to meet these changes effectively?

3. Of the nine kinds of people in VALS, which are you most likely to attract?

4. Read Luke 14:28-30. Name a specific change you would like to see your congregation make and a specific cost you expect it to exact.

Notes
1. Peter Schwartz, *The Art of the Long View* (New York: Doubleday, 1991).
2. Stanley M. Davis, *Future Perfect* (Reading, MA: Addison-Wesley Publishing Co., 1987).
3. Arnold Mitchell, *Nine American Lifestyles* (New York: Warner Books, 1983).
4. Michael J. Weiss, *The Clustering of America* (New York: HarperCollins, 1988).
5. Ibid., p. 4.

9

....

POINTERS FOR PARADIGM LEADERSHIP

Effective leaders help people experience their future before they live it. Leaders who are able to manage paradigm shifts must learn to make others comfortable with a vision of the future. In this chapter, let's examine some of the skills required.

SPEAKING PICTORIALLY

Good paradigm managers recognize that groups think with their emotions, not just their intellect. Especially in the Church, people need to have paradigms presented with emotion, not just the facts. This requires the special language of imagery, of parables, of folklore, because these styles of communication speak not just to the head but to the heart.

In their wonderful book *The Language of Love*, Gary Smalley and John Trent write:

An emotional word picture is a communicative tool

that uses a story or object to activate simultaneously the emotions and intellect of the person. In so
doing, it causes a person to experience our words,
not just hear them.[1]

New opportunities require new word pictures, described in
ways that are vivid and easily recalled. Effective paradigm
managers look for pictures that help turn concepts into
actions. Folklore, metaphors and anecdotes are vital tools of
the trade.

When a church is in the process of change, a good word
picture is like a welcome visit home. It enables people to
anchor the future in the familiar. It communicates by means of
a "down home" word picture they already recognize.

Bill Hybels presented the mission of Willow Creek
Community Church by using the picture of "unchurched
Harry." Everyone felt they knew "Harry," and as a result every
member of the church can picture its exact mission by the
mere mention of the name. A simple word picture has been
articulated so effectively that the newest visitor and the oldest
veteran share the vision.

Others have used the phrase "the rock generation" to articulate a mission to reach baby boomers and baby busters. This
picture allows immediate recognition of the target group. For
some, the phrase conjures up a mental image of Woodstock.
For others, it's U2 and Aerosmith. Innovations from contemporary culture applied to church life are immediately understood in this picture.

The Power of Anecdotes

We have found anecdotes to be an effective way to lead our
church to visualize our reason for being. We wanted to
express ourselves as an outreach-oriented church in an environment of love, acceptance and forgiveness. We needed sto-

ries and word pictures to fix this vision in the minds of our members.

One of my favorite stories along this line is of a person who once came to a staff member wanting to identify all the divorcees in the church. The staff member wisely said, "Absolutely not! We don't check anything at Eastside."

He went on to say, "Why don't we just hang placards around the church on Sunday morning, and have everybody sit in sections identified by their former sins? You know—ex-thieves, ex-liars, and I suppose we would need a section also for present liars."

This is a great story to express what we mean by an environment that is committed to love, acceptance and forgiveness. This anecdote is deliberately repeated two or three times a year. It immediately retrieves for members the mission and battle cry of our church.

The Role of Folklore

Churches have folklore, just as families do. The folklore in my family includes the story of my grandfather loading five kids in a black Model T Ford and driving from Iowa to Washington during the Dust Bowl. I can still visualize the photos of my father with his old-fashioned, depression-days clothes hanging in the back of the car. In his hand, he held one of those little caps that thugs wore in movies of that era. In my mind, I can even see how he folded it.

How beautiful and adventurous my grandmother looked, dressed for travel across the plains. My grandma and grandpa once recollected how they had picked fruit when they arrived in Washington state, just to survive. It is amazing to me how often I still think of the stories they told of traveling across the country. They sparked a permanent sense of adventure in my heart.

This is the kind of folklore that bonds families and churches.

The great Roman orator Cicero said that word pictures are "lights that illuminate truth." He told his students, "The more crucial the message, the brighter the lights must be."[2]

TAKING TIME TO WORK ON YOUR MENTAL MAPS IS ESSENTIAL TO STAYING ON COURSE. FORGETTING TO DO THIS CAN CAUSE YOU TO END UP IN THE DUMPSTER.

Anecdotes, folklore and metaphors give power to paradigms. Storytelling personalizes our mission and establishes memorable patterns for the future.

OPTIMISTIC LEADERSHIP

Paradigm pioneers are optimists. Because optimism and pessimism are also a part of our emotional makeup, your anecdotes will reveal whether your view of the future is optimistic or pessimistic, anxious or reassuring.

Obviously, effective paradigm pioneers communicate optimistic visions of the future. Telling stories that relate dark and frightening events of the past is no way to motivate people to look forward to the future. Surprisingly, optimists tend to be more realistic than pessimists, according to author Martin E. Seligman. Pessimists, he says, may be accurate prognosticators simply because they cause their own worst scenarios to be fulfilled.[3]

An optimistic leader:

- Has the conviction that the future will have a positive outcome;
- Communicates a sense of competency in facing the future;
- Views testings and setbacks as problems to be solved and "courses" in which to learn more in the university of life.

Church life has a way of knocking the optimism out of us. Leaders know what it is like to deal mostly with problems week after week. But optimistic paradigms can provide a clearer picture of the church to help us refocus on our mission and to fortify us for the tough times. Taking time to work on your mental maps is essential to staying on course. Forgetting to do this can cause you to end up in the Dumpster.

My old friend, the late Jamie Buckingham, used to have a plaque over his typewriter that read, "Whom God loveth He beats the heck out of." That line contains a lot of truth. Sometimes God may lead us through the dark valleys because He wants to toughen us.

Positive paradigms are essential because people are worn out by the negative. They come to church pressed down with bad news from television and home life. Their boss has informed them they haven't reached their quota. Their kids are telling them what parental jerks they are. Paradigm leaders learn to positively entreat their followers with word pictures of achievable aims.

If you are afraid of the future, how can you possibly come up with solutions for the problems you and your church face? This doesn't mean you expect everything to be perfect. The church world is often compulsive about this, expending far too much energy on being right. The point is that an effective leader must develop "solution-sensitive thinking," confident in God's power to enable him or her to meet the future, however imperfect it may be.

When a church has been presented with positive paradigms, it knows its aims well enough to have confidence that new crises can be avenues to greater effectiveness instead of threats. The belief that crises and problems open the door to success propels people into the future, filled with spiritual power. When the Church's mission has been presented effectively, small failures become the building blocks to greater success.

THE GIFT OF CRITICISM

Leaders who dare to propose a new paradigm naturally leave themselves open to criticism from the defenders of the status quo. We had better learn to be comfortable with criticism or we won't last long! I don't like being criticized anymore than anyone else, but I am learning to be fairly good at receiving it because I know that criticism presents my greatest opportunities for growth. Joel Barker writes:

> Here's a good first step toward paradigm pliancy: when someone goes against your paradigm, fight your natural tendency to explain why it is impossible, and, instead say: "I never thought about it that way before, tell me more." And then, be quiet and listen. You will be surprised at how many good ideas you will hear.[4]

Above all, avoid the fatal flaw of meeting criticism with the insistence that "God has told me that this is the way to go." I have learned never to say this, especially in times of stressful change. It may quiet some in the congregation, but unless you have 100 percent accuracy in hearing the voice of God, you'll pay a dear price. I would rather say, "We are going to try this, and if it works we will know it is God's will. If it doesn't work, He'll let us know that He wanted to teach us something."

Criticism can help to focus on paradigms and give them the kind of rigorous analysis they need. Untested commitments

IF WE EMBRACE CRITICISM INSTEAD OF RESISTING IT, WE MAY BE PRESENTED WITH NEW OPPORTUNITIES OF SERVICE THAT IN TURN MAY OPEN UP VISTAS OF SUCCESS WE WOULD HAVE NEVER SEEN WITHOUT CRITICISM.

rarely become reality. Patience and the willingness to have a paradigm questioned can enable you to respond to genuine concerns and make necessary adjustments.

Some time ago at Eastside, a woman dropped a critical note into the offering plate. At first it looked like a petty complaint—the kind that, I admit, annoy me. Fortunately, I avoided the temptation to send off a snappy response and decided to give her a phone call instead. I was humbled when the woman began to apologize for what she now viewed as a cranky note. When she explained, my impatience changed to compassion.

The woman was in the latter stages of leukemia. She just hadn't been feeling good about anything, including worship. I empathized with her and prayed with her. Then I invited her further criticism. Her specific complaint was that our information booth outside the auditorium was inadequately staffed and allowed too many people to be backed up. Seven or eight people were standing in line, and she had to wait for quite some time to ask her question. She informed me that three or four people left in frustration without getting the information they sought.

This critic's perspective let us know that unless someone was unusually patient they wouldn't have the stamina to work through some of our systems. We were not consistently expressing our paradigm of care. We believe that laypeople can do that kind of ministry better than paid staff, but our logistics weren't demonstrating that belief. So we corrected it, employing some of the ideas the woman suggested.

If we embrace criticism instead of resisting it, we may be presented with new opportunities of service that in turn may open up vistas of success we would have never seen without criticism.

Leaders who are friendly to criticism develop the skill of:

- Nondefensive learning;
- Seeking to understand more than being understood;
- Deliberately collecting critics who help them spot opportunities.

Unfortunately, few churches I know of invite or value criticism. But criticism isn't an enemy if your paradigm is firmly in place, reminding you of where you are headed.

APPLYING PARADIGMS TO PATTERNS

Although we take such single complaints seriously, regardless of tone, we rarely act on them as we did in the case of the woman who had difficulty getting information. We have, however, learned to watch for patterns in complaints. When we begin to see patterns in the critiques we receive, we quickly move into an action mode.

How do we discern such patterns? For one thing, we make it a regular practice to collect evaluations from our volunteer workers. We also pursue input from the newest among us, who often have the ability to see problems that veterans miss.

The value of discerning patterns is that they often reveal future trends. Many exciting new tools have made collecting trends an easier task in our time. I have found George Barna's writings on trends particularly helpful in training laypeople in the importance of trend watching. (See *The Frog in the Kettle* and *User Friendly Churches*, both published by Regal Books.)

Nearly every community in the United States has applicable data for trends up to 10 years in the future. These are usually available at your chamber of commerce, government agencies or organizations such as Barna Research (write Barna Research Group, P. O. Box 4152, Glendale, CA 91222-0152).

Trend watching in a local church can be fascinating. At Eastside, we once went through a season of 70- to 80-year-old men coming to Christ in unusual numbers. What were we doing that was allowing us to be effective with elderly men? We never could find a reason, but finally concluded it was prayer (probably the prayers of their wives who were having to live with them in retirement!).

We also try to spot trends in our Sunday School attendance. We can tell that we have a paradigm weakness when our people are unwilling to invest in the young people of today.

We pay close attention to attendance in our Church 101 course, our primary means of describing our mission. If our volunteer numbers drop, we know we are not getting the message across that we are a lay-driven church, and an outreach-oriented church especially concerned to reach baby boomers and their children.

Watching trends can help assess your effectiveness in presenting paradigms and offering programs. Leaders who ignore patterns and trends cannot ethically blame the church for not responding to their leadership.

TECHNOLOGICAL TRENDS WE FACE

In his book *Life After Television*, George Gilder anticipates an era that is fast approaching.[5] In the next few years, the fiber-optic systems that telephone companies are beginning to install will offer unprecedented opportunities and challenges.

In the world to come, according to Gilder, the influence of television networks and cable systems will be drastically diminished. He predicts that the people who are now attending our churches will be able to "call up" television shows anytime they want.

Think of it: no video player required, no having to learn how to set the clock on that crazy thing! Simply sit down at the keypad and send a message through the optic line requesting "I Love Lucy" at 5:00 A.M.—or church time—and within seconds it's yours. Myriads of educational programs will be at everyone's fingertips.

This is going to radically change the way people think—including the way they think about the Church, and especially about preaching. Many preachers have just begun to come to grips with the way television has reduced the average attention span. Some say it's no more than seven minutes, and with the new technology's endless variety of options, it will likely become even shorter. And audiences will probably become even more oriented to listening only to that which meets immediate felt needs.

Much of our training in the future will be done through video banks. We'll get entire degrees without leaving home. We are having discussions in our leadership teams already about opportunities this could offer. Fiber-optic connections could allow our congregation to meet at several places at once with interactive television. I wonder if larger churches in the future won't be meeting in multiple locations. Who knows— maybe we will have pastors pastoring multiple churches hundreds of miles apart. You never know! The opportunities are definitely broader than we can imagine.

The advancement of technology in one field will lead to many others. One discovery gives rise to four others never thought of. Accelerating change is a safe prediction.

These new technologies will force upon us new paradigms of what we mean by church. And they won't all be negative. Wouldn't it be refreshing if we had paradigm pioneers prepared to seize the future?

PATTERNS IN GIVING

Pastors know the importance of watching the pattern of giving in the church, but not everyone realizes how this is changing. Most churches operate on the premise that 20 to 25 percent of the people carry 80 percent of the financial load. This is likely to change in the future, however, especially in churches that have a high percentage of boomers.

Often in seeker-sensitive churches the giving pattern is more like 15 percent of the people carrying 80 to 90 percent of the financial load. Spotting this pattern can help you better understand the paradigm of skepticism that pervades the boomer culture. We need to have new understandings of money and the Church. We need to have new paradigms about what offerings mean. We need new metaphors to tell the story of the importance of fund-raising.

Normally, we have thought of financing churches in terms of general budgets set by "the management." It is easier to do it that way. And it gives missions organizations, children's homes and other ministries a relatively stable source of financing. Trends among boomers, however, show that they will give to specific persons, projects or challenges before they will give to a general budget.

I know that this can be maddening to a leader. It is to me. But it forces us to be more creative in presenting needs. It challenges us to discover the particular people who are open to contributing to specific ministries. We are finding that some people are willing to fund facilities. Others want all their contribution to go to missions, others to youth ministries or outreach ministries to the community. Boomers don't possess a high level of loyalty to institutions.

OTHER TRENDS TO WATCH

The future can never be flawlessly predicted—partly because the pace of change in our culture is at quantum speed. Yet, some changes on the horizon are of special interest to church leaders.

Having church leaders who are unmarried is one of them. Churches often don't know how to commission single men and women. We have treated singles as an aberration for so long that we have lost perspective. Nearly one-half of the adults in the United States are single. We will see more and more single men and women becoming pastors and leaders in the church. Will we be prepared for this small shift?

The "green" movement—sensitivity to the environment, and against physical, audible and visual pollution is going to affect the Church more and more. We already see opposition to large church buildings in city after city. I'll be surprised if these trends change. The NIMBY (not in my back yard) syndrome affects churches, too. Big developments on the west coast are no longer considered a plus, but intrusive.

Many anticipate that when baby boomers move into retirement, the Church will see an unprecedented resurgence of missions. We are seeking now to develop concepts within our church to seize this force. New paradigms of what we mean by missions and missionaries need to be created now.

These and other changes impose themselves on the way we define ourselves. Leaders who can anticipate trends optimistically and energetically will be ready to seize the moment. The effort to try to imagine your future is time well spent. It may allow you to anticipate problems and prepare new ways of curing ills. New lenses can be prepared to see new realities. New rules of the game can be spotted before the game changes.

TESTING OUR ASSUMPTIONS

Assumptions are what we have already decided to be true—presumptions we make about reality. But isn't it embarrassing how often we find that our assumptions are wrong? Assumptions must be tested and changed as the evidence requires. This can be done in several ways.

Stick to the Data
Willingness to track data is the first step. Good paradigm leaders *look* for ways they can be proved wrong. I constantly want to be introduced to reality. Not long ago my assumption about how Eastside grows was challenged. Although we were determined to grow through reaching the unchurched, we discovered that much of our growth has been through transfers from

other churches. This is in direct contrast to our mission.

At least twice in our history, tracking data has uncovered new challenges to do better at tending to real needs. On the surface, we seemed to be successful in achieving our paradigm of church, but in reality we weren't.

I was once working through our budget for the coming year. We had been assuming that about 20 percent of our attenders contributed 80 percent of our budget. As I was totaling a category of expenditures in outreach, I began to question this percentage. I felt we had advanced in the area of discipling but I wasn't sure how much.

I asked our data-processing people to collect some data on ratios. Sure enough, our assumptions were very wrong. The data told us that 33 percent of our church was carrying 80 percent of our financial load. This time the news was good; we were doing a better job at discipling than we had assumed.

Look Through the Eyes of Others
Nothing is more dangerous for paradigm pioneers than relying only on their own point of view.

For example, many people need to question their assumptions about how the unchurched might receive the gospel message. I transitioned into a whole new world when I began to listen to secular people who were not necessarily antagonistic to church life. My assumption of antagonism was totally wrong. Most secularized people today have tasted the rotted fruit of secular humanism and are open to other paradigms. The vast majority of people are friendly to faith. Most churches don't believe that there is a relatively high level of genuine interest in the gospel. I began telling positive anecdotes and stories that reinforced our paradigm to be an outreach-oriented church. We consciously dismantled assumptions that those outside the Church hate our message.

Another dangerous assumption is that people must feel guilty before they can fully receive Christ. Our experience is that repentance usually follows an understanding of grace. It's parallel to the man born blind in John 9. Only after Jesus healed him was he moved to return and manifest the fruit of repentance by giving thanks.

As one man put it, "You preachers don't understand—you can't feel bad until you feel good." Jesus came bearing grace and truth. He first extended grace to His listeners, then they were able to repent and listen.

Try driving to your church sometime pretending to be someone else. What do your signs look like? Can you find your way to the rest rooms? Does the facility flow toward the auditorium or is it hard to find? What would it be like to be a single pastor in your church?

Try "Possibility Thinking"

What would you do if you had a million dollars?

Are you sure you don't have as much money as you need?

What if 50 percent of your community all at once wanted to attend church?

This kind of thinking can lead to some interesting possibilities that challenge the socks off the things you assume to be true about yourself and the people you lead.

Collect dissimilar opinions. "Antithetical thinking" can lead to the golden solution. What is the opposite way of doing what you are presently doing? Try it on in your mind for a while. Discover some of the disadvantages in the way you approach ministry. This kind of thinking can open new pathways into the future.

Reading a variety of books and magazines broadens possibilities. Perhaps you should also go outside the arena of the Church. One of the most beneficial experiences I have ever had was interacting with a secular sociologist about our community. He offered many ideas on how we could achieve our goals that I would have never thought of.

COMMON ERRORS IN INNOVATION

"Innovation-friendly" churches run into common pitfalls. A few of these are dangerous enough to warrant some explicit warnings.

Error Number 1: The Copycat Syndrome

I have attended seminars taught by the best. I've heard presentations on everything from preaching to taxes, all taught by famous authorities. I loved the way most of them communicated. Unfortunately, I sometimes come back to my own congregation and try to imitate them. I fail every time I do this. The people back home view me as somewhat supercilious.

One day as I was preparing to head off to another conference, one of my leaders said, "Oh no, is this who you are going to be now?" naming the famous preacher who was leading the seminar. His comment crushed me. Then I realized he was right.

We can learn from a lot of fine models and gain a great deal of inspiration from others. Inspiration is vital. Learning and developing an arsenal of possible solutions to problems you face is very helpful. But there is only one you. Copying the latest fad without processing it through your own good, hard thinking can only lead to problems. The copycat syndrome destroys your own authenticity.

When you attempt to apply any new information or insight to your church, the Holy Spirit ought to be intimately involved in the process. Only He can blend what you have learned with His will for your own personality. If you simply copy from others carte blanche, you will only disorient your people. They will view you either as artificial or meandering with your current hero.

Good leaders are open to being influenced by others, but they remain authentically true to their own calling.

Error Number 2: Failure to Collaborate
Paradigm-sensitive leaders are people who have the patience to share in collaborative leadership. The old autocratic style of leadership will simply not work in our time. The effective leader of today will develop the skills required to enable a group to think *together.* You need to be able to depend on a team of several coleaders who hold to a common paradigm.

Working through two or three separate groups of leaders on vital issues to the church can raise the odds for success. If you are going to significantly change any portion of your church, the failure to collaborate will be a costly mistake.

Following are some team-building approaches to collaborative leadership.

- Invite lay leaders to collect research on how churches change. This may take several months, but it will be time well spent.
- Discuss the possible financial effect of a paradigm change with those in your church who have financial expertise.
- Share the concept with core leaders. In a church of 100 this may be as many as 20 people.
- Elicit feedback from large numbers of people by mailing out questionnaires that invite personal interaction.
- Review the effect of the change with a small group of leaders—those who would be responsible for implementing the new idea.

- Seek consensus among this group on how the first step ought to be taken.
- Announce the decision to implement the new direction at least six months in advance. Allow a one- to two-year test period.
- Celebrate progress along the way with the entire church and recognize the workers who have made the progress possible.

NEW IDEAS REQUIRE FAILURE TO BE PERFECTED. IT TAKES AN IMMENSE LEARNING CURVE TO MAKE ANY VITAL CHANGE IN THE LIFE OF A CHURCH.

If the pastor in the anecdote I used at the beginning of this book had taken these steps, I wouldn't have received that call from his bishop. By giving just a little attention to collaborative leadership, the pastor could have been a model of change for his bishop.

Collaborative leadership is not standing in front of a group with a blank sheet of paper to be filled in. The people in your congregation rightly expect you to have a sense of direction. Collaboration is sharing a direction about which you are thoroughly informed and to which you are committed. Its aim is to give ownership of any changes to those who will have responsibility for them and be affected by them. People work hard on a project in which they have a vested interest. Boomers are particularly dispassionate toward top-down direction and leadership. In the final analysis, it takes the whole church to implement new paradigms.

Error Number 3: Underestimating the Learning Curve

New ideas require failure to be perfected. It takes an immense learning curve to make any vital change in the life of a church. Don't ever underestimate its size.

Everyone must expect struggles and setbacks. If not, despair and discouragement will prevail. Discouragement can be a tough enemy to progress. Unlike dissatisfaction, discouragement is never a beneficial tool. The word itself describes why. Discouragement is a compound word composed of *dis,* meaning to take away, and *courage*—which comes from the Latin word for heart. Discouragement, therefore, means to dishearten, to take away one's courage. Facing the future successfully requires courage.

It took our congregation years to fully arrive at our vision for the kind of church music on which we would focus. Often, I was in travail. Frankly, in our attempt to be creative, we had a lot of stupid music. Sometimes it was horrendous. When we began to see hundreds of unchurched people attend services, our worship collapsed. We were doing stuff that was so off-track it made us look as though we didn't know where we were headed. Yet, gradually, our learning curve improved. Now we have a team of dozens of people who know exactly what our format is and where we are headed. They have observed and benefited from the learning curve.

Anticipating the learning curve allows people to feel better about failure. Knowing that we expect them to fail allows people to be more adventuresome.

The temptation to abort most new paradigms is strong. Perfectionism snuffs out creativity before it gets started. Creative realism fills what we are trying to do with joy.

Error Number 4: Failure to Connect with the Past

Often young leaders will launch out on deliberate paradigm shifts and have little sensitivity to the history of the group they are leading. For example, I received a call from a church leader asking me how to get his church enthused about evangelism. I asked him what he meant by that. I discovered that one of our former leaders had become part of the congregation he was leading. They determined after reading some of our materials that they were going to reach baby boomers, and in a big way! The problem was that the preponderance of the church members were not boomers.

The church had been very successful over a 20- to 30-year period. I encouraged him to lead the church through its successful history—to show them how their willingness to innovate in the past was still a call today.

Any change in a group without a tie between what has been and what lies ahead will seem like an indictment rather than a vision. Affirming the value of where the church has been should be the first step in every attempt to introduce change.

A leader must find the points of continuity between the past and the present. The first place to begin may be to rehearse the vision of those who have gone ahead. Then, begin to show how the vision of the future is consistent with the Spirit's work in the past. I honestly feel it most often is. No one has ever been truly original. God uses the building blocks of yesterday to build ministry today.

Taking time to compare and contrast paradigms to introduce people to new methods requires great skill. When that skill is developed, change in the local congregation becomes much easier.

PARADIGMS *in* PRACTICE

1. Can you visualize a change you would like to make in the church, as an animal? For example, would it make your

church a roaring lion? A busy beaver? Experiment with more than one animal metaphor.

2. Think of a story or anecdote from the pages of your church's history that would make a good bit of folklore to remind your church of their vision and identity.

3. Do you view yourself as a pessimist or an optimist by nature? What experiences have helped shape this outlook on life? How can a firm faith in the resurrection of Jesus help shape one's outlook?

4. Make a brief list of things you assume to be true about your church. Now try and find data to prove them. Talk with others to see if they share your assumptions.

Notes
1. Gary Smalley and John Trent, *The Language of Love* (Colorado Springs: Focus on the Family Publications, 1991), p. 20.
2. Ibid., p. 21.
3. Martin E. Seligman, *Learned Optimism* (New York: Alfred A. Knopf, 1991).
4. Joel Barker, *Future Edge: Discovering New Paradigms of Success* (New York: William Morrow and Company, 1992), p. 109.
5. George Gilder, *Life After Television* (New York: W. W. Norton and Co., 1992).

10

....

THE CHANGE PROCESS

THE NATURE OF INNOVATION

Not long ago, I was looking for a book I was certain I'd stored in our garage attic. I put the ladder in place and headed up to search for it. My only certainty about its location was that it was in one of 20 boxes. I was dreading the search.

I never did find the book. Instead, I had a trip down memory lane. I found my son's first baseball glove, and I relived all those years of umping and trying to catch curve balls. I tripped over an old snowsled I'd had since age 10. There, too, was my grandad's old mason's chisel.

I found several books I wasn't looking for. I sat down on the dusty floor and just flipped through them, noticing my highlights and reading my own notes. I climbed down the ladder with six books tucked under my arm—none was the one I was looking for, but I was glad I'd found them, nonetheless.

Some of these old forgotten thoughts were jewels I would have gladly purchased. But they were already mine.

This is exactly the way we should experience innovations. Everything we need to do has already been done. Innovations should take us down memory lane in a new way. Innovation should ring of history. It should sound like something we've heard before, and yet it should be different.

GUIDELINES FOR INNOVATORS

Churches and church leaders can be taught to view innovation as positive. Here are some guidelines:

1. Remember that the Church has been at its best when it encouraged innovators.
2. Recognize the value of the testing process. Give innovation a chance and then evaluate.
3. Separate ideas from people.
4. Remember that anything that is for the cause of the kingdom is for Christ and for us.
5. Thank God that He gives the Church people who will look under rocks previously left unturned.
6. Don't take new ideas as attacks on your own.
7. Count the cost. Don't start until you know the real risk and expense.
8. Honor present commitments.
9. Celebrate variety. Stay young. Spend time with young people.
10. Develop a philosophy that views change as having the potential to make things better.
11. Be humble. Don't be a know-it-all. Say, "Let's see if it will work," not "God wants it this way." Even innovators aren't always right.

12. Await confirmation. See if there are other people who see what you see. If no one in the church agrees with you, you are either extremely far ahead and need to slow down, or you are wrong.
13. Get people's permission before they are in a position to have to pay the price. Sometimes innovators aren't those who pay for the innovation. But giving permission for innovation and then helping to pay the price creates team players.

One of the most innovative and alive people I've ever met was the late Dr. J. E. Orr. I believe he held more than three Ph.D.s. When he visited our church he was working on a Ph.D. in Education at UCLA, unbeknownst to his family. (I promised I wouldn't tell.) He was also learning to use computers years before young people discovered them. Dr. Orr was in a perpetual learner's mode. He was enthusiastic about checking out any new move of God he heard about. He criticized and cheered people on at the same time.

I am planning to live into the next century, should the Lord tarry. My prayer is that not only will I see, but also encourage, innovations that will contribute to influence the Church. I hope a few won't be easy for me to grasp because then I'll be sure to grow, too.

Sustained plateaus of growth stagnation in a church can destroy its heart. Change is always a by-product of healthy growth. An unbending commitment to the status quo is the first sign of death.

I also think "change for change's sake" is a worthwhile consideration. A sense of freshness often allows the opportunity for people's faith to increase. However, change must be managed. A clear understanding of paradigms and the change process can help you prepare a church to move through change joyfully.

Steps in the Process

Several steps need to be considered in preparing your congregation to move through change by using paradigm technology. Of course, some change can be induced merely by crisis, but it is healthier to endeavor to manage change by these steps.

1. Discover Present Paradigms Held Dear

A consultant friend was working with a major denominational church in our area. They had filled the facility to capacity on Sunday mornings. The usual suggestion in such cases is to have multiple Sunday services. My consultant friend, however, quickly realized that the primary paradigm of this church group was *family*. The church not only viewed itself as a family in the spiritual sense, but also most of the people were related to each other. Many of their businesses were interrelated in the community as well. The group feared that any change in the church's meeting times would threaten this sense of family.

The group also had a strong sense of local mission, but the primary paradigm of the church as a family was in conflict with their desire to do outreach. Opinions and felt needs were colliding all over the place. Their ideas of a successful church called for mission without growth.

The consultant made a good effort to encourage the congregation to develop two services, but one of the elders said, "You don't understand."

"What do you mean?" the consultant responded.

"You just don't understand what we are as a church. We are a family."

The consultant queried, "Can you explain what you mean by family to me?"

"Happily!" the elder continued. "For 25 years I have eaten

breakfast with Aunt Lydia and Uncle George before the Sunday morning service. Then three generations of us gather inside for a barbecue or other meal after the service. It's been the same families meeting together for 25 years. We can't change this. This is who we are."

Now, a novice consultant may have tried to assault this paradigm. My friend, however, realized that the identity of this church was set in concrete. After thinking about the situation, he offered a way for the church to achieve their mission and still maintain their identity. He suggested that they raise funds to build a new facility that would accommodate everyone at once. The church members were very excited. They had found a way to accommodate their vision and burden for outreach without giving up their identity.

The first step in dealing with this congregation was to discover what paradigms its members held dear. Often, younger leaders in particular fail to appreciate existing paradigms. Such previous commitments must be celebrated! Sometimes they can be applauded for the innovation they represented in their time. Affirming the past can be an important step in the process of change.

2. Show Continuity with the Past

Certain traits in existing paradigms can often be identified as important stepping stones toward the future. Let's say a congregation finds itself surrounded by baby boomers, while the church itself is populated with people age 60 and older. By making an appeal to reach a lost generation, and possibly by showing how this same congregation was mission-focused in the past, an innovative leader could give the church a goal for the present that is consistent with the past.

Again, suppose the planned innovation is to move from a single pastor to multiple pastors. The value of the ministry of the church's previous pastor can be emphasized, then the value-added dimension of his having assistance can be shown.

We went through this in our own congregation. There was some shock when we began to add one and then two pastors. This occurred first when we were at about 300 to 500 in attendance. At first, I could sense the congregation having great difficulty with their feelings. They liked Mike and Jerry, our two new pastors—in fact I think many felt disloyal to me for enjoying them! I gave place to the two new men as speakers and the church began to grow accustomed to them. I also expressed a great deal of appreciation for the relief I felt by having such strong help. We consciously reinforced our philosophy and mission. Eventually, the congregation saw how the present could embody more of the advantages they had experienced in the past.

3. Nurture a Hunger for New Opportunities

Choosing the leaders who surround you is very important. Leaders who model a sense of adventure are healthy in times of change, while maintenance leaders who hold rigidly to past structures aren't that helpful. The more adventurous of your team should be the most visible in these times because their enthusiasm will create enthusiasm in others.

When our leaders wanted to adjust our services to a more seeker-oriented format, I took at least six people to Willow Creek Community Church in North Barrington, Illinois. When we watched the drama sketches oriented to the unchurched, they understood what I had been talking about for months. The effect of this trip worked exactly as I had hoped it would. It began to nourish a hunger in our significant leaders to reach out to the unchurched. I also invited those who were the best at reaching the unchurched to address a core group of leaders. By having encounters with those who had gone ahead of us and accomplished our previous dreams, we were able to create confidence.

4. Locate Models of What Lies Ahead

Finding groups with whom to network is vital. When we hear of a church that has dealt successfully with financial stress, we send out a team to study what they have done. We have networked with those who have dealt effectively in mentoring lay leaders. Models are worth 10,000 words. Sheer exposure to other paradigms of what a church is and methods they have used in solving problems can enhance the repertoire of any congregation.

Exposure to new ideas also spawns a creative mentality in a church. This may be one of the most vital ingredients in successful change—if the right people have the exposure. We send too many professionals to leadership conferences. Our vital lay leaders too often get left out. They wonder what in the world we are talking about. Then we pastors wonder why they can't follow us. Often the problem is that we have seen the model while they haven't. Networking laypersons is a necessary investment.

One helpful pointer: Prepare the group before they go to the seminar. Give them an eye for what you hope they will see. Also, encourage them as adults to give their honest feelings when they return. Post-trip debriefing can be as vital as preparation.

If your church numbers 200 and you are wanting to break that threshold, find 400-member churches with which to network. If a style shift or generational shift is in order, invest time in finding models before implementing change.

5. Use Vivid Word Pictures

In our church's setting, we have come to avoid words such as "evangelism." We call it the big *E* word because so many people react negatively to it. Most laypeople freeze when you mention evangelism. So we say we are "bringers and includers." That seems much more natural and doable.

When you find a phrase that defines your new paradigm vividly, stick to it. People are easily confused. In times of change, it is all the more important to stick to consistent par-

....

OUR CHURCH'S EFFORT IN MAINTAINING OUR COMMITMENT TO THE LANGUAGE OF LOVE, ACCEPTANCE AND FORGIVENESS HAS LENT ITSELF TO GREATER STABILITY IN TIMES OF CHANGE. WE HAVE KEPT IT SIMPLE, SUCCINCT AND CONSISTENT.

....

adigm word pictures you have used in the past. If terminology changes in times of crisis or change, the group can be shaken and rattled. We have spent a great deal of effort in maintaining our commitment to the language of love, acceptance and forgiveness through the multiple shifts our congregation has seen. I believe this has lent itself to greater stability in times of change. Keep it simple. Keep it succinct and consistent.

6. Spot Paradigm Tension Points
At least three major paradigm tension points can threaten innovation. You can count on them, and you will do well to prepare for them.

The cut-expenses versus growth mentalities. In my experience, there are two basic kinds of leaders. Some—usually laypersons—want to trim expenses in order to deal with inadequate resources. Others want to acquire more members—even if it means spending money to do so.

We have found that cutting expenses usually doesn't enable the church to move ahead aggressively. But a good leader is able to adapt to both approaches when reality requires it. Both mentalities are needed in the church, even though they frustrate each other. It's a predictable point of tension.

Pre-1960s versus post-1960s age groups. The potential tension between those born before and after the '60s cannot be overstated. Although we are a congregation that is clearly committed to reaching the baby boomer generation, we feel this tension acutely from time to time.

Boomers are action oriented. They are visual and sensual in their approach to decision making. Boomers want to be part of a winning team. Their parents (the pre-'60s people) involved in church life tend to be more conservative. They are far more loyal to institutions and careful about doctrines than boomers.

A boomer will choose orthodoxy and action over wise process. The Truman generation is reluctant to face too much innovation. Neither of these perspectives is good or bad. They are simply realities and paradigms of reality.

Many an unwitting leader has had an innovation scuttled by this conflict. My book entitled *The Baby Boomerang: Catching the Baby Boom Generation's Return to Church* (Regal Books, 1990) could be vital reading to those who are leading a pre-'60s congregation and want to transition into effectively reaching the post-'60s generation.

But it isn't just baby boomers' parents who can be sensitive about change. I learned the hard way that boomers are just as capable of being locked in the past. We had a Christian rap music ministry with our kids. One of the boomer parents came to find me following a meeting.

"Pastor, don't you think the volume is too loud?" the mother, who was in her late 30s, said. Her tone of voice sent the message, "Please agree with me, Pastor, so I can go kill that youth minister."

"Well, it's a little louder than I like," I agreed, "but it seems to be filled with lyrics about sexual integrity, honesty and seeking Christ. Better yet, the kids understand it better than they would if I had played a few tunes with my guitar." I laughed. She didn't.

"I think rock is OK, but that kind of rap music is on the radio and it pushes killing and mistreatment of young men—don't you see anything wrong with it?" She stopped. I felt she was honestly asking me to help her see what was going on.

"Well, Elaine, do you remember when you were in high school?" I paused.

"Yes!" she answered.

"Were you a Christian?"

"Yes." Her eyebrows were rising. She knew I was making a point she wasn't going to like.

"Did you like church?" I cleared my throat.

"No, I didn't like it at all." She was getting the picture now.

"You see—I'll bet you didn't understand it. It probably went too slow for the way you learned. And the styles were just a bit out of synch with your tastes. We want to reach these young baby busters. And they listen a little bit differently than we do. We're wanting to create an environment where the Lord owns rap and whatever else is the communication channel of choice to these young postmoderns. I want to give them an opportunity to experience Christ in a cultural form they understand."

"I think I see what you're getting at," she said, "but don't you think the youth pastors need to watch very closely the influence of this stuff?"

"I promise: they do—and I do."

I happened to know this young woman had been vitally

involved in the Jesus People movement. She was as radical as anyone. In fact, she still perceived herself as an innovative Christian. How quickly we forget.

Seeker-focused church versus Christian-focused church. This is the toughest tension with which to deal. All Christians have a way of defining themselves as normal. Our definition of normal is the standard by which we judge others. Yet, realistically, none of us is normal. We are all unique.

Still, any church that exists for any period of time will gradually slide toward caring for its clientele. This stymies outreach. John Wesley anticipated this "slide up" as the end of all revivals. Especially in times of change, those who hold paradigms that are more outreach-oriented will have conflict with those who want to major on nurturing Christians. Sometimes this tension is insurmountable, and it becomes advisable simply to encourage a mission outpost church.

If you want to encourage a paradigm of church success that depends on reaching the lost, the strength of your paradigm presentation will determine the degree to which these tensions can be resolved. Resist the temptation to meet objections by doing battle personally; view them as philosophical differences.

7. Allow for Dialogue

A wise leader will subscribe to a basic, three-step process in presenting any new direction to the church.

- Explain your paradigm to the core group.
- Collaborate with the committed workers.
- Share with the entire congregation.

Open dialogue is vital to a successful change process. Baby boomers, particularly, don't want a "mandate from the mountaintop." They want to think they have participated in the process of discovery. Boomers don't want to follow the dreams of a leader; they want leaders who are serving their (the boomers') dreams. And because the boomers are coming into cultural dominance, the days of people identifying so thoroughly with a strong leader that they give their lives and gifts to his or her dream are likely gone for many decades.

Questionnaires and small-group interaction are essential methods of dialogue. They help develop a collaborative environment, particularly in times of change. If you are moving from a maintenance- or nurture-oriented church toward an outreach church, you may have a tough period of dialogue ahead. Moving from a Truman-generation-based ministry to a ministry to boomers is even tougher.

I have developed a practice of opening our Wednesday night service with a question and answer time in which we encourage questions about our church life. I have encouraged an environment where we can have "right spirited" criticism. I may ask how changes that have been presented have affected our congregants, and how they might affect other people we haven't thought of. This interaction allows me an opportunity to evaluate change that might be occurring.

This process has introduced many good ideas. We changed to one midweek service a month as a result of such sessions and have three other midweek evenings devoted to small groups.

At one of these dialogue sessions, a wonderful man who was clearly committed to our church said bluntly, "Doug, you obviously don't take spiritual input in the lives of our junior highers very seriously." Of course, I was stunned by his statement, but everyone sensed sincere emotion in the comment. I also sensed some pain that needed to be addressed publicly. I paused before I responded, reaching for an extra measure of grace.

Finally, I asked, "Could you clarify your statement? Are you asking why we don't have activities for junior highers on the other three midweek evenings in the month?"

The inquirer said, "Yes. My kids have nowhere to go three weeks a month. We love this church but we are worried about the spiritual input into their lives."

"You have hit on a valid point we hadn't thought of," I admitted. "I'll take your concern to our leadership team, and we'll come up with a solution to this."

Our solution was to have an event for junior highers several times a month. We developed a team of junior high lay leaders and a group of drivers for transportation. The criticism was a first step to better care. It allowed us to adjust to everyone's benefit. Allowing for criticism and critique improved the acceptance level of our primary paradigm. It also increased the sense of ownership by the entire church.

8. Use Multiple Channels of Communication

We have discovered that it takes us at least six weeks to get across even the simplest announcement to the entire church. I believe this is true of most churches in excess of 200 attenders. Churches of less than 200 need repetitive channels of communication to get across any message as well. And more and more, people are expecting highly sophisticated and competently produced communications.

Printed material that begins to state the change process is essential. Clear and concise graphics, charts and diagrams can be helpful. Remember, most people today are visually oriented.

Emotional communication is essential as well. A great way to think about any form of communication is to ask yourself three questions: What do I want the people to feel? What do I want them to know? and What do I want them to do?

Show in your communication that you have tested the factuality and the validity of this change. Then present the outcome you hope the new paradigm will achieve.

Video is a vital way to communicate in our highly visual-
and audio-oriented times. Today, churches of any size can use
video. Its cost is going down in price yearly. (Eastside has
videos available. See the back of the book for catalog information and the address.) Other forms of communications
technology will be essential in the technologically astute generations that lie ahead. The use of technology is a major paradigm shift itself.

DON'T SIMPLY TALK ABOUT NEW PARADIGMS. LIVE OUT PARADIGMS WITH ACTION! CELEBRATE ACTION!

Cassette tapes are another great way to communicate information. We use cassette tapes several times a year when we
want to introduce new programs or enhance the shared paradigm of what we mean by church. I got the idea from a teaching tape by Peter Drucker. Numbers of churches are doing this
effectively. Because most people have cassette players in their
cars, this form of communication can be used by the businessman driving across town and the family on vacation. And
this may be a surprise: Cassette tapes can usually be prepared
less expensively than brochures.

Using multiple ways of conveying information assures that
your message will be carried on multiple wavelengths. Also
use multiple emphases and styles. Share the process and pro-

cedure of changes the people can expect. Explain how you came to these decisions. Give colorful anecdotes and utilize humor in explaining changes. Let people sense it, taste it, feel it and see it. Make it a full-orbed communication event for them.

9. Enact Changes

Action! Action! Action! Leadership is action! Baby boomers especially want an action-oriented church life. They will become frustrated in an overly process-oriented church. Too often, churches simply talk about being good but never are. They discuss doing but never do.

We often employ a phrase that has been made famous by business consultant Tom Peters: "Ready, Fire, Aim." The phrase implies that in certain situations it is better to enact a change too soon than to wait too long. Have a definite start date and stick to it. And don't forget to celebrate the action when you begin.

If a congregation, for example, wants to inaugurate an alternative service to reach baby boomers or busters, it is important to set an exact start date. Announce it three to four months ahead of time, and fill the church's communications channels with it during the last six weeks before the date.

Then, as the Nike ads say, just do it.

Don't simply talk about new paradigms. Live out paradigms with action! Call the church to action! Articulate action! Showcase action! Display action! Celebrate action!

10. Celebrate the Fruitfulness of Change

As we have already mentioned, it is important to report to people the fruitfulness of the efforts they have put forth. Much church fund-raising, for example, is ineffective because we never report back to people what we have achieved with the money they have given.

Celebrate goals even when they are not achieved. Celebrate how close you came to achieving them. Or celebrate everything you learned by not succeeding!

11. Develop the Story for Future Pilgrims

I find it helpful to several times a year retell the story of the beginning of our congregation. I am amazed at how people who have joined the church after its beginning point love to hear how we began in our living room with 10 people.

I also like to tell about the day our church burned down. We were nomads moving around in our community while our building was being reconstructed. Later journeyers celebrate with us these stories that are vital to our church life. In the stories, we find the heart and core of our church. More than anything else, groups use folklore to enable themselves to face the future and to deal with problems.

Tell key stories about when new members and staff members joined. Your own congregation has many such tales if you look for them.

I regularly tell the story of our 12-step programs. I inform everyone why we started them. We didn't start the first one because every other church in town had one; we began it in self-defense. We had so many people needing support and help in escaping addictions that we began a whole program based on the needs that presented themselves. Hence, I am able to present our leaders' thinking not as professionals who know exactly what to do but as bumblers in the Holy Spirit who are trying to find a way to be effective.

12. Clearly Define Changing Roles

Churches need pastors who have clear job descriptions. If a clear job description isn't communicated, the people will supply dozens of paradigms of their own about what they expect of a pastor. Developing metaphors that present definitions of your role as a leader helps the multisensory communications receptors people have today.

Answer questions such as: What will the change require of the pastor as a leader of the people? What will this change require for other professional staff? For lay leaders? For the people themselves?

The following word pictures were developed initially by John Wimber, pastor of Vineyard Christian Fellowship in Anaheim, California. We have applied them very effectively in critical times of change and adjustment in our church, as have many others.

Compared to baseball. A pastor may move from a player to captain and then to coach. Then he may move to manager, general manager, owner and league president.

Which of these baseball metaphors describes your present role as a church leader? Do you see any approaching changes in your role? Do you think that any of the above word pictures could enhance the way your congregation understands your role change? How will you prepare your church to accept this change?

Compared to ranching. This is another word picture often used to present the process of growth in a church. Using this metaphor, a pastor may describe himself as an apprentice hand, ranch hand, lead hand, foreman, rancher, then ranch owner.

An apprentice hand does all the dirty work. I have effectively used this metaphor in describing to the church how my wife and I did 90 percent of the ministry when we started the church. Obviously, as the church grows the metaphor must change. What will happen in the future if your church grows by several hundred people and you are still trying to do all the dirty work? It's likely that you will need to change to being a lead hand or foreman.

How will your role in the church change as you add staff

members? You may move to the role of foreman, to rancher and then to ranch owner.

Remember, such metaphors enhance paradigm shifts, allowing for changes in:

- The lenses through which reality is viewed;
- The rules by which the game is played;
- The boundaries and definitions of success.

Using word pictures to describe changes in your role as a leader can release others to participate creatively in the change. They can also enhance your own perception of your changing role and enhance your own growth. And I believe that most successfully negotiated growth thresholds have at their core the leader's own growth.

PARADIGMS in PRACTICE

1. What shifts in roles would you as a leader need to anticipate if your church were to grow through the following size thresholds? What metaphors would you use to describe each new role?
    a. 100-200 attenders
    b. 300-400
    c. 500-700
    d. 800-1,200
    e. 1,300-1,900
    f. 2,000-3,900
    g. 4,000 and above

2. Scripture uses several metaphors to describe the Church. It is said to be the Body of Christ (see Eph. 1:22,23); His bride (see Rev. 21:2); people bought with a price (as redeemed

slaves, see 1 Cor. 7:23; 1 Pet. 1:18); a temple (see 1 Cor. 3:16); the household (or family) of God (see 1 Tim. 3:15).

Which of these metaphors would best enhance the paradigm you see for your congregation? Would some other metaphor fit better? (Are you primarily a hospital? A fellowship?)

3. What role do you see for the pastor's wife in a church of 100-200? Of 500-1,000? Of 2,000 or more?

4. What role for small groups do you see for a church of 100-200? Of 500-1,000? Of 2,000 or more?

5. An effective leader once said, "Do today what you will need to do when the congregation is larger, and it will grow larger." What changes would you make if your congregation were twice the size it is now? Which of these changes would be good to make now?

11

....

WRITING YOUR
FUTURE AS HISTORY

I've made friends with eight raccoons. Our house is on the development line of greater Seattle so we see deer, coyotes and raccoons regularly. Most evenings, after everyone else has gone to bed, I spend an hour or so with these raccoons.

It's relaxing and a nice break. They eat out of my hand and a couple of them let me pet them. Three members of the clan are the most notable: the young raccoon I named Tommy; Big Jack, a 40- to 50-pound male who travels alone; and Momma. I first met Momma a few months ago with her three young raccoons. She got to know me and made sure I fed her kids every night.

Tonight as I was writing, Momma showed up alone. I thought I had seen one of the kids traveling with a group of four adults last night so I wasn't surprised if she was by herself. I looked up from my computer and there she was, standing on her back legs, peering up at me through the glass. She looked so alone. But it was time for her kids to move on.

Several months ago she wouldn't let them out of her sight. Now it was time for change.

That's the way with nature. It rises and falls in cycles, confronting us with the new and asking us to say good-bye to the old. Letting go is part of life.

Leaning back in my chair, I searched for a way to describe how it feels to a church when they know they must change. I think we feel the way Momma did. We want to keep what we've had, but sooner or later it is time to let go. We can't fight the flow of time any more than Momma can fight the cycles of nature.

The way we worship needs to be evaluated regularly and changed if necessary. The procedures for choosing staff and supervisors ought to be reexamined. The balance in our mission needs to be scrutinized to see if we are meeting real needs and being faithful to our calling as the people of God. We need to let go of many of the ways we do things and look forward to who our future will make us.

PARADIGMS AND THE FUTURE

Tell me the paradigms that define you and your church and I can tell you a great deal about your future. As we have said, paradigms are lenses through which we view reality, and your lenses will determine what you see. Paradigms set boundaries, and that will determine predictable limits for your church in the future. And, as rules of the game, paradigms can tell you what game you will be playing.

You may have a building plan displayed in your foyer, but it is not nearly as good a predictor of the future as the word pictures that describe the church's primary paradigm. Let me in on your word pictures and I can tell you where the church can be in 10 years.

How you define your target audience will tell me the nature

of your attenders (if you are consistent with your focus). If I can pick up on how you talk about people, I can tell you whom you're likely to reach. "They" and "them" statements will assure me of the people you will be excluding. If you talk about "those" people with abuse problems or substance problems, it tells me that your future will not include many people who struggle with addictions. On the other hand, inclusive pronouns—"we" and "us"—will define your future as one that

STANLEY DAVIS CONTENDS THAT AN ORGANIZATION'S FUTURE EMERGES OUT OF ITS "VIEW OF WHAT IT WILL LOOK LIKE IN THE FUTURE."

includes people who have a variety of needs.

I am not being egotistical about my predictive abilities. You could make the same kinds of predictions based on what we've covered in this book. Defining your present picture of successful ministry will allow you to work toward future aims.

How do you define a mature Christian? What does the end product of your church look like? Do you choose status quo, change-resisters as leaders? This would assure me that your future will be filled with limited innovation but a great deal of security. This is neither good nor bad. It is simply a statement of fact. If, on the other hand, you value entrepreneurial types as leaders, your future will probably include more innovation and the church will be more likely to seize opportunities.

We have referred to Stanley M. Davis's book titled *Future Perfect*. In it, he challenges institutions to write their future ahead of time. Davis contends that an organization's future emerges out of its "view of what it will look like in the future."[1] His insights have considerable application to Christian leaders. He challenges us with the need to arrive ahead of trends by using the following application of sound and time:

> Sound travels at the speed of about 660 miles per hour. Think of two airlines, one sub-sonic and the other super-sonic, travelling from point (1) to point (2). The sound emitted from the sub-sonic plane reaches point (2) at the same time that the plane does. The super-sonic plane, however, reaches point (2) before its sound does.
>
> Imagine arriving in a plane at point (2) and then waiting for the arrival of your sound. In this context, you are there before the fact. You have created a phenomenon, gotten ahead of it after it was created and observed it catch up with you.
>
> This is strategic leadership. Developing concise paradigms for your future is a vital part of this kind of leadership.[2]

INNOVATIONS AS RESPONSE TO NEED

We are all familiar with the way innovation is often viewed as a threat. The fact is, it can be a source of security because it prepares us to deal with groundswells of needs that are already occurring. Peter Drucker suggests:

> Strategic leadership that will ask questions in uncertain times can prepare itself for success. Matching a company's strengths to the changes that have already

taken place produces, in effect, a plan of action. It enables a business to turn the unexpected into an advantage. Uncertainty ceases to be a threat and becomes an opportunity.[3]

There is an art to bringing order to the chaos of change. Drucker contends that all innovation, rather than being the developer of history, is a reaction to history. Smart leaders sense the reverberations that lie ahead and develop scenarios of response. Unfortunately, the reverse side of this principle was illustrated when the Berlin Wall fell. Suddenly, unprecedented mission opportunities lay before us in Eastern Bloc nations. Yet, few churches and mission organizations were prepared to really take advantage of the window of opportunity quickly enough.

Drucker maintains that the invention of the computer, rather than being the driving force in the information age, may in fact have been a product of the increasing hunger for information. The real causes of change may be discovered by hindsight.

Although Davis refers to this kind of thinking in the business world as "future perfect," Drucker calls it survival.

Can we live in the future perfect? And can we see order in chaos in times of uncertainty? Is your church comfortable assessing its strengths?

Keeping the End at the Beginning

What is a Christian? What an obvious question! But it is surprising the variety of answers one can tally from it. Try another question: What is a *mature* Christian? Such questions about the end result we envision for our work are important to keep before us at all times.

Widely known minister Howard Hendricks has taped to his pulpit a poignant phrase: WHAT ARE WE TRYING TO DO TO THESE PEOPLE ANYWAY? The point of his reminder is to preach to an aim. When organizing a church's vision or structure, it is essential that this question be kept at the focus of your discussion.

The guy in the grey coat asked me, "Now, what are you really trying to accomplish here with people?" Then he took a sip from his Dr Pepper soda. *A typical sociologist's question,* I thought to myself. We had hired this doctor of sociology to help us.

"We want to reach them for Christ!" I replied.

"Yeah, I know that," he answered seriously. "But what are the behavioral changes you want to see? This will help me as I evaluate your progress." It was refreshing to see a serious member of his profession at work.

"Well," I answered, struggling for a more specific response, "we want to bring people into spiritual life through Christ, where they develop a relationship with God."

"Well...see, I'm not a Christian so that doesn't make much sense to me. What specific, observable things would I do as a Christian? What would you have in mind as a successful Christian?" he pressed. He looked up through his glasses, hoping I was on track with his questions.

"Oh! I see what you're getting at. The question is, What does a mature Christian do? You want to know what behaviors we want to instill in people as devoted followers of Christ?" I hoped I was tossing the ball back in his court.

"Yes, now we're on course. It seems to me that not many of you Christians are comfortable being very clear about your aims," he finished. He then began writing on his notepad and preparing for further discussion.

My friend, the sociologist.

I thought the answer to the question, What does a mature

Christian look like? was obvious to the point of pain. But most of us never stop to give a specific definition of the end result of our work. Our preaching, our self-definition and expending of resources should go toward the aim defined by our understanding of a mature Christian.

About a year after my encounter with the sociologist, we set out a simple definition of what our aim was for every person who would become a devoted follower of Christ in our church setting. We want those whom we disciple to:

- Read at least five chapters of the Bible a day;
- Have a growing relationship with Christ in sharing and prayer;
- Have a clear grasp of the basic, orthodox statements of the Christian faith and be able to apply them to their personal lives;
- Become members of a small group that meets twice a month;
- Attend at least three to four public worship settings a month and apply the truth to their personal lives;
- Share their spiritual gifts with the congregation and their financial resources in tithing and offerings in the work of the Lord;
- Experience the joy of Christ in an atmosphere of love, acceptance and forgiveness;
- Become bringers and includers, knowing how to invite people into their life in Christ and include them in their hearts.

These are statements used to define our target in those who join us at Eastside. Knowing our goals increases our effectiveness. I would encourage all churches to hammer out a similar list.

ESSENTIAL ELEMENTS OF YOUR HISTORY

In order to write your future as history, you must give specific attention to several key elements that are present in any group endeavor.

Define Your Target Audience

Your paradigm of an effective church naturally defines your target audience. Working by objective requires thoughtfulness. Paradigms that match the needs of those the church wants to reach are necessary tools. "Niche-marketing"—aiming at specific people groups—is essential in today's segmented society.

Ask What Should Never Change

Let's emphasize again that although target audiences may change, and methods must change, core values must not change. Biblical values must remain constant through all paradigm shifts. For example, we can never change our commitment to the Bible as the authorized and infallible word of God and the final guide for the church. Preaching, teaching and proclaiming the Word are all unchangeable focuses of a church that is faithful to Christ.

The value before God of every individual over and above the institution, over our strategies and visions, will also remain an unchanging priority for us at Eastside.

The church I pastor is committed to youth as a priority. It is unwaveringly committed to outreach in an environment of love, acceptance and forgiveness.

The incontestable basics define the starting point of all change.

Dump the Baggage

Most of us can think of present realities that are in the way of tomorrow's fruitfulness. You may not be able to change these roadblocks for a number of years (or maybe never at all), but at least being able to assess the obstacles can be an important part of the history of your progress.

I know of a church that after critical assessment closed its doors. The administrator had stolen a six-figure amount of money from the church, causing it to lose a great deal of credibility. The leaders felt they were unable to move beyond the "distrust factor." Closing down was a courageous step. People who have been betrayed often aren't likely to be innovative in the future. They needed healing. There are higher values than keeping the doors open.

As we have noted, at Eastside we had to deal with the view that assimilating new people was unsatisfactory and unworkable. In order for us to move into the future in an inclusionary mode, changes were in order, and changes we made.

A congregation in a medium-size city once invited me to speak at a special occasion—their new evening service for baby boomers. They were planning a gathering of several hundred people who were enthused about an expanding vision for this mainline church. Many of the people hadn't wanted to go to a boomer service but now were glad they had done so.

I asked the pastor how he was able to ignite such rare enthusiasm about a rock-generation service in a traditional church.

"Well," he began, "first I had to convince them that our style of worship with a classical organ and two hymns was baggage in reaching young families in our community." He spoke quickly and with excitement. "I knew they valued the idea of reaching out to all these couples, but they didn't want to change the service. So we listed everything that was an obstacle about what we were doing," he finished.

The classical organ and two hymns were dropped, and the people came.

On the way home, one word stuck with me. Baggage! Once they identified the baggage they were willing to let it go.

What baggage has Eastside picked up in our journey? I asked myself.

It is a good question. It is one I keep asking.

Ask, "What Are We Good At?"

Excuse the grammar, but it's the most direct way to get to the point. There are many things that our church isn't good at. But there a few that we are good at. I'm certain it's the same for you.

It is entirely possible to build a vital and healthy congregation with any number of emphases. What you are good at is defined by your gift mix and proven by experience. Being aware of what you have been good at is the key to understanding your future.

What are the clear needs in your community that your church is already good at meeting? Could you continue to meet them in the future by expanding the parameters of how you minister to people?

In 1991, we hired the services of Barna Research Group to do an analysis of unchurched people within five miles of our church. We found three primary kinds of meetings that unchurched people said they would attend. One, they said they would attend a seminar on time management. Two, they said they would attend a musical event. Three, they said they would attend something like a movie or similar entertainment. Four, they would attend something that was related to families.

We began to analyze what needs we were already good at meeting in each of those categories. We set about to devise strategies to help us capitalize on what we were already good at before we added new programs.

With the Lord's blessing, it has worked.

Define Future Leaders
In writing your future, include a chapter on the skills that will be necessary for someone to be a leader in your church. How would a good leader be defined 10 years from now?

Without doubt, leaders define a church's personality. The mentality of a leader toward people, toward the Scriptures, toward Christ, sets the tone of what the church will be in the future. By outlining your aim and training your leaders for the future, you could outline a curriculum for training leaders for the years ahead.

> # MAKE YOUR FUTURE HAPPEN. WE MUST BE IN THE DRIVER'S SEAT, WRITING OUR FUTURE AHEAD OF TIME.

How we define leadership today will define our church culture in the future. Multiple leaders in the church is a possibility for our future. Leaders of the future are likely to be more and more specialized.

Leadership is the single-most scarce resource in the church today. This is a matter for serious prayer.

Safeguards to Remember
Successful churches and leaders not only set out toward the future with a positive attitude, they are also aware of pitfalls and corresponding safeguards. Following are a few to keep in mind.

Avoid the numbers game. It is easy for numbers to become

the singular definition of a church's success. It is my personal feeling that growing churches are at least 80 percent luck—or the result of the Lord's singular and sovereign blessing—and 20 percent skill. Maintaining growth once it begins is 100 percent character.

Warnings are in order both for churches that grow and those that don't grow. I have seen an equal number of churches frustrated at both ends. Growth is frustrating most of the time. Not growing can be even more frustrating.

Don't be victimized. Make your future happen. Don't just let it happen to you. Too many leaders are not anticipating what lies ahead. Too many are not developing alternate scenarios for projects they initiate. Good management involves paradigm preparation. We must be in the driver's seat, writing our future ahead of time.

Much of the time you will not be in control of forces that influence your congregation and your life. To avoid being a victim, you must determine to be in control of the way you respond to such forces. By avoiding a victim mentality, you'll be more effective in facing the unexpected.

Don't stand alone. Developing a network of friends experiencing similar circumstances is like a parachute. Find successful models either in your own city or around the country. Many times I have heard leaders talk about the network of people who have been vital in their lives and in the success of their congregation.

Jamie Buckingham was this kind of friend for me. Before he died in 1992, Jamie often served as someone with whom I could depend on to network—not just to pat me on the back but to also serve as a friendly critic. Recently, I asked myself if I had found another critic. Although it struck me that Jamie is irreplaceable as a person, I need a replacement who can take up the role Jamie played.

This need is partly why my wife and I joined a small group.

For several years we had talked about small groups, and suddenly we realized we weren't practicing what we preached. So we joined up. Our small group has become a valuable time when we can be human and vulnerable. Fellow journeyers make the journey fun and allow us to take surer steps. Having a rope tied to you from time to time as you go out into adventurous realms can bring a sense of security.

This is true for churches, too. It helps to know someone else who is "trying this stuff, too." Your people need fellowship with other churches who hold similar paradigms. I have discovered from experience that you may find more in common with a church similar to yours in size and mission than with a church of your own denominational affiliation.

The point is that we need one another as never before. We all have lessons to learn from a network. We all have homework to do if we want to write our future as history.

Paradigms in Practice

1. What is your church's primary strength? (What are you "good at"?)

2. List some community needs you would like to see your church meet.

3. Now, match your answers to 1 and 2. Could any of your church's strengths give it a "cutting edge" appeal if developed?

4. What about your church must never change?

5. What "baggage" would you like to see your church leave along the way?

6. What traits of a church leader do you see your church needing in 10 years?

Notes

1. M. Davis, *Future Perfect* (Reading, MA: Addison-Wesley Publishing Co., 1987).
2. Ibid., p. 38.
3. Peter Drucker, *Wall Street Journal*, Cover Page, 1992.

12

....

FUTURE OPTIONS AS OPPORTUNITIES

If the variety of paradigm options has you in shock now, just wait—there will be more in the future. But remember: Strategic paradigm thinkers see new opportunities and discoveries in every crisis. They leave it to others to bewail possible problems and to wave the flag of fear as their basic form of communication. Good leaders see new challenges as possibilities.

CHALLENGES AND OPTIONS AWAITING THE CHURCH

Multiple Models of Successful Churches
During seminars about reaching baby boomers, I've detected tension between pastors of various sizes of churches. Pastors of large churches are reluctant to gain lessons from smaller congregations, and pastors of smaller churches are often hesitant to apply the methods of a fast-growing large church.

Our future will demand the unity and tolerance to accept

multiple models of church. Many different sizes of churches will need to emerge for us to be effective in reaching our nation. Multiple models will be required to fit multiple needs and opportunities.

I am astonished that in an area as small as the greater Puget Sound, where I live, so many models of church life are required to be effective. Some pockets in our community are

VISIBLE COLLABORATION BETWEEN MEN AND WOMEN IN CHURCH LIFE MAY BE ONE OF THE GREATER OPPORTUNITIES FOR EVANGELISM AHEAD OF US.

totally blue-collar. Others are totally white-collar, upper-management, highly educated. In the inner city, entire sections consist of yuppie urbanites. Every major locale faces this kind of variety—along with the same opportunity for multiple focus.

Women in Leadership
The expanded roles for women in our society have affected American culture forever. The church cannot be naive about this. Our culture at large is highly sensitive to women's rights, complaints and issues. Across the country, more and more women have qualified themselves for leadership. Yet, the Church has few paradigms that allow for women to be preachers, spokespersons and leaders.

Galatians 3:28 asserts that in Christ "there is neither...male nor female," but I am amazed that utilizing the gifts and talents of women in leadership is still considered controversial by some. The ban against female leadership is a part of the nonnegotiable elements of many churches' paradigms. The apostle Paul's desire for women to be veiled in Corinth (see 1 Cor. 11:5-16) is ignored, while his statement that in that particular cultural setting they should "be silent" is universalized!

Visible collaboration between men and women in church life may be one of the greater opportunities for evangelism ahead of us.

Baby Boomers in Leadership

Over the next 20 years, baby boomers will replace their parents as predominant spokespeople for Christianity. I am not so sure we will see many stars such as Billy Graham rise on the horizon. We are more likely to see innovative experiments as the focus of this generation. As boomers move into prominence and power in the political arena, they will also begin to rise in prominence in the church arena.

But the million-dollar question is, In which churches? Fellowshiping groups such as the Calvary Churches, and other more casual groups, are the kind of models that will likely become dominant in the future. Some regions are more formal than the west coast, and perhaps less open to this style of church. But many traits in such churches will cause boomers everywhere to flock to them.

It is difficult to predict what changes boomer prominence will bring during the next 10 to 20 years. It is also difficult to predict whether most churches will make the effort to include the boomers. It is my fear that if we don't become more effective at reaching this generation, the counterspirituality of non-Christian religious movements may outperform orthodox Christianity among boomers.

The Appeal of Medium-Size Communities

In the state of Washington, we have been observing growth in many midsize communities. Having new communications systems available in the home in the form of fax machines, computer networking and, on the horizon, fiber-optic connections, medium-size communities may be the growth focus of our future. Our state has been called a "bellwether state." So if the past trends hold, people will be moving to medium-size communities. I have read a variety of projections, but one is certain: New churches will be needed in communities of this size across our country.

Smaller or midsize communities represent the desire for a slower pace. Can local congregations in urban and suburban settings offer some of the appeal of small communities? I think they can. We'd best be careful about overemulating megachurches.

Increase in Property Expenses
Can we have "church plants" in the future such as the ones we have erected in the past? I don't think so. In our community, land and construction costs will prohibit our ever being able to build a facility large enough to house the fruitfulness of our congregation. Large malls and huge church plants will be the kinds of expansive development denied in many "green" and ecologically committed communities.

The sheer cost of building facilities has gone up so astronomically that I find congregations everywhere have no hope for their own building. Our community code requires three acres of land on which to build a church. Three acres in one of the medium suburbs of Seattle could cost $1 million and up. We have calculated that it would take a congregation of 300 to 400 people to be able to afford the land, let alone build a building and make the payment on it or raise the funds for it.

Of course, we do believe in the miraculous touch of God on our churches and we are hoping that baby boomers will actually tithe to the churches to which they belong. Yet, present trends preclude such optimism.

As positive paradigm leaders, what kinds of solutions should we seek? Large churches can be downsized. Multiple campuses of a single large church can be considered. More and more churches of 100 or less will be meeting in nontraditional and less expensive facilities. Medium-size churches that have traditional—and costly—facilities will be seriously challenged.

In our church planting, we are suggesting that pioneering leaders consider organizing for the first two years in groups of 12, meeting in home groups three or four Sundays a month and gathering in one assembly only once a month. This allows a preacher to produce only one smashing sermon a month. The once-a-month public service can also be a great seekers' event, including a music program developed and organized to attract the target audience. Also, small groups can develop the relationships necessary for the larger church's life and health.

It is our feeling that too many resources, and too much money, are spent unnecessarily on facilities by churches that have memberships of 10 to 40. This size congregation will have fewer and fewer available resources in the future. The sheer debt load boomers are carrying will inhibit their ability to contribute significant sums of money to their worship sites.

New models will arise. We should celebrate, anticipate their coming and encourage anyone with an innovative idea.

Churches for Seekers
What kind of church will the unconvinced attend in the future? Innovations for attracting seekers must be encouraged. In a society that is clearly in a post-Christian era, we will need to be much more friendly to churches who are focused 100 percent toward a seeker population. Although basic, orthodox doctrine will never cease to be important, seekers will not be patient with some of the doctrinal nit-picking that is prevalent in many churches. Seeker-centered churches can develop two focuses—one that is highly visible and seeker-centered, and

one that is behind the scene, oriented to nurturing committed Christians. Churches for the unchurched are needed to revitalize our influence.

Lay-Driven Ministries
Interactive communications are likely to open many new doors for training lay leaders in our church. The growing

> ## We will need to put away our gospel guns and celebrate anyone who is effective in winning people to Christ.

technological expertise of our culture will create two phenomena: More and more people will expect a high level of technology in the church, and the ministry of these laypeople will need to be celebrated.

The Growth of Process Evangelism
In the past, many churches became accustomed to "crisis evangelism"—a presentation of the gospel that results in a relatively dramatic conversion. In the days to come, we will be challenged to accommodate conversions that are more of a process than a crisis. We will have in our ranks people who are friendly to the gospel, yet not persuaded enough to make a dramatic decision.

Accommodating this "preconversion" phase stretches many congregations. I am not comfortable with it. For me, receiving Christ was a crisis experience. Yet, I have many friends who insist they have received Christ but cannot name a specific moment of crisis when they did so.

How to deal with the whole issue of evangelism will be vital in our future. We will need to put away our gospel guns and celebrate anyone who is effective in winning people to Christ. The challenge to communicate the gospel in a variety of methods lies ahead of us.

Charismatic/Pentecostal Influence

Almost all large evangelical churches have charismatics in their midst. Why did they leave their Pentecostal/charismatic home? Being a charismatic, I can say that many did so because many charismatic congregations became preoccupied with extreme discipleship stances or failings because of other extremes.

For whatever reasons, charismatics have become "main-lined." Their openness and exuberance in worship and their acceptance of the gifts of the Spirit represent a treasure chest waiting to be opened.

A friend recently said to me, "Your congregation is much more friendly than Pentecostals and charismatics these days." (Keep in mind that we are charismatic.)

"Well," I replied, "you must have changed a great deal."

"No," he responded (keep in mind that he is not a charismatic). "You charismatics have calmed down a great deal."

The benefits of the Pentecostal/charismatic movement are beginning to be appreciated across the world through what Peter Wagner calls the "third wave." I predict that the wave will continue and that ways to appreciate the gifts and calling of the Holy Spirit will contribute to the lay ministry movement in the Church.

Our God is the God of creativity. He is also the God of prophecy. And as He promised Amos, He won't do anything unless He first reveals it to His prophets. A prophetic, Spirit-led people can more effectively seize the future than those who rely on their own efforts.

A PARTING WORD

At the end of the twentieth century, the opportunities far outweigh the problems. But the Church's future leaders must think boldly and creatively. They must be deliberate managers of paradigm models. The most effective congregations will be those that can state clearly what they will be in the future. Their leaders will be able to articulate paradigms and encourage paradigm shifts that will function as effective and faithful models, lenses and rules.

Of course, much that lies ahead in the next two decades is unpredictable. But the thoughts and exercises we have outlined in this book could allow us to traverse some rocky seasons and seize upon some very fruitful opportunities—and some fun times as well.

The younger need to celebrate the accomplishment of their elders. The older need to make room for the younger innovators. The less adventurous need to thank God for the pioneers who are willing to risk placing their necks on the chopping block. And those that are more into risk-taking need to accept the fact that there is a place for consolidating our gains.

All this will take bighearted people—the kind in whom God's own great heart can richly indwell. It is my hope that this book on paradigms and leadership will contribute to this end.

PARADIGMS *in* PRACTICE

1. In your vision of the future, what size congregation will be best?

2. Where are you and your leadership team on the subject of women in leadership roles?

3. How do you feel about the possibility of a church without a large facility of its own?

4. Do you think that the "process" model of evangelism and conversion can be accommodated in a church that is accustomed to the "crisis" model?

5. How do you feel about the Church's need to access the gifts of the Holy Spirit today?

Continuing Education for Church Leaders.

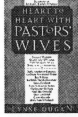
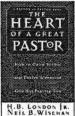